Real Estate Investing Online for Beginners: 3-Hour Crash Course

Build Passive Income From Home

Edward Day

Table of Contents

Introduction

"Never depend on a single income. Invest to create a second source." -Warren Buffett

Real estate investing is one of the most profitable and secure sources a person has in order to build their wealth. The real estate market has returned an average of six to eight percent every year over the past century. Despite the housing market crash in the previous decade, real estate continues to be a great source of wealth for Americans.

One of the biggest advantages of investing in real estate is that it allows you to build your wealth while you sleep. Passive income is a holy grail for many people, and rightly so. You don't need to put in additional work to earn it. You place money in it and it goes away and grows itself, without needing any major inputs from you.

As wonderful as passive income sounds, it can be tough to earn it. There aren't many sources of it and the ones that are easy to execute tend to pay a pittance. For example, a savings account generates passive income. However, it pays you an average of just 0.5% per year in the United States.

That's less than the rate of inflation. In effect, you're losing money by opening a savings account! However, it is still better than having all of your money in cash. Real estate investing is so powerful because it allows you to grow your money passively, without having to worry about inflation, or other economic conditions, that will reduce the value of your investment.

We live in increasingly unstable times. The world is changing far too quickly for us to be able to comprehend what's going on. During such times, you never know when your primary source of income will get disrupted. You could fall victim to automation or your entire industry could be rendered obsolete.

Having a secondary, passive source of income is essential to deal with these times. Real estate investment is the best way forward when it comes to building such an income stream. There's just one problem.

Where do you find the money to invest in real estate?

Online Real Estate Options

One of the biggest hurdles people face is that real estate investing requires a lot of money. If you're looking to invest a $100,00 home, you're going to have to put $20,000 down if you're approved for a conventional mortgage. You could seek an FHA loan and put just $3,000 down, but closing costs will push even this to the $5,000 mark. This isn't chump change that people have lying around.

However, investing in physical real estate gives you a lot of advantages. For one, it's good to have the security of knowing that you have something of your own in case the worst happens. Owning the property directly means you'll never have to worry about having a roof over your head. The stability that it brings will help you make positive changes in your life, and it's something that everyone yearns for. It's just that the money involved puts it out of reach for most people. The average person saves for years to be able to make a down payment.

There's also a little secret that gets brushed over by most real estate investors. When you draw a mortgage, even if you earn rent from that property, you're effectively flushing your freedom down the drain. Think about it. Most mortgages have 20 to 30 years terms. This means you've adopted a constant cash outflow for the next two to three decades.

Sure, it services an asset, but this constant cash outflow can be tough to manage if times turn rough. There's also the fact that being a landlord isn't easy. It's a full-time job, and if you hold down an existing job, that rental property can turn into a nightmare if you end up with the wrong sort of tenants.

Physical real estate provides a lot of tax relief options to make up for all this hassle, and it remains a great option for people looking to build their net worth. It's just that net worth and liquid cash are two different things. For example, a person who has one million invested in stocks has more buying power than someone who has a million tied up in their home's value.

The latter cannot withdraw that million to pay for anything. The former can sell their stocks to receive cash and reinvest that into other opportunities, this is what I meant by freedom previously. You'll be giving up some flexibility when you invest in physical real estate. Some people are okay with this. They don't mind the negatives as long as the positives manifest themselves. However, some people are not suited for it.

What if there was a way for you to combine the advantage of real estate investing with the flexibility of the stock market? This is where online real estate investment comes into the picture!

Truly Passive

The internet has opened the world up in so many ways. These days, it is possible for you to invest in real estate online, without having to leave your home! One of the options in this book has existed since the 1970s, but a few of the other options you're going to learn about are recent developments.

Even if you wish to buy physical real estate, there are many other options to invest in properties at the click of a button. You can gain access to detailed financials as well as learn all about neighborhoods and their relevant statistics. You can speak with sellers online and prepare offers here as well. The days of kicking the tires before purchasing a property are long gone. I must mention that this is the case with turnkey rental properties.

If you're looking to become a rehabber then you will have to view the property physically. Aside from physical property, there are online-only options that eliminate the high barrier to enter the world of physical real estate. The options you'll learn about in this book will help you invest in real estate no matter how little your capital is.

I'll also be showing you how you can turn your rental property into a truly passive stream of income. This is something that most landlords don't consider doing because they have preconceived notions of what being a landlord involves. I'm here to save you from a lot of unnecessary work!

So who am I and why should you be listening to me?

Who I am

You already know that my name is Edward Day and my official job description reads 'full-time forex trader.' I live in Chicago with my wife, two daughters and two dogs. I enjoy the good life as much as any reasonable person does. These days, I'm lucky enough to have a vast portfolio of investments, but this wasn't always the case.

I graduated college with a Master's degree in accounting. I worked at a stable job as a Chartered Accountant for a while. I enjoyed the security but truth be told, it was hard for me to believe that this was all there was to life. I felt that there was so much more I could be doing.

The markets always interested me, and it just so happened that one of my clients was a forex trader. He invited me to a seminar, and it's safe to say that I was hooked. I began devouring all the forex trading knowledge I could find after that, and I even went back to university to work on a Bachelor's degree in economics.

I found that I had an intuitive feel for the markets, and in 2008, I quit my job to focus full time on trading forex. I haven't looked back since. While forex provides me with tons of active income, I have built up a portfolio of passive income producing investments.

I have been investing online in real estate and have managed to earn a steady 12% return on average since I began doing it. I'm often invited to speak at forex trading seminars, and I manage to pass along a few real estate investment tips as well.

The advice you will read in this book is derived from real world investing experience. I'm not going to tell you anything about investment opportunities that I haven't personally tried before. You're getting the real deal with regards to all of these opportunities.

While my personal experience will color some of my views on these investment avenues, I've tried to be as objective as possible. My focus is to educate you about the tools you have available at your disposal so that you can make the best decision possible for yourself.

The time has come for you to stop using a lack of money as an excuse to avoid real estate investing. It might be a little intimidating but I assure you that you don't need a high IQ or some special degree to learn this stuff! The best time to begin is right now.

So, let's dive right into the subject of online real estate investing!

Chapter 1:

Why Real Estate?

Before getting into the details of how to invest in real estate, it pays to take the time to understand why real estate is such a profitable investment. For over a century now, real estate has been one of the primary drivers of wealth in America.

A big reason for this is the government's push to ensure that buying a home is as hassle-free for

Americans as possible. This means the average real estate investor has a ton of options when it comes to financing and purchasing properties. The tax breaks that real estate ownership provides also plays a major role in enhancing wealth.

Let's first begin with the absolute basics. What is real estate? Real estate refers to a tangible property. This could be a building, a home, a commercial facility or even raw land. The key market of real estate is that it is attached to something physical.

For example, if you buy farmland, you can earn money by growing crops on it. However, you own the land that produces the crops no matter what. This tangible asset ownership is what separates real estate investment from other avenues such as owning stocks and bonds.

A stock is an ownership in a business. This business has its own economics and operates based on these. Its prospects ebb and flow and depend on the overall economic cycle of the sector it does business in. Let's say the worst happens and the business goes bankrupt. In this case, the shareholders usually don't receive anything.

This is because the creditors of the business have first say on the assets it owns. This leaves the average shareholder with a lot of risk during bad times. The investment value could go to zero and often, shareholders are left holding the bag with nothing to show for their money.

Real estate is similar to stock investment in that it provides you with two avenues to earn gains. You can grow your money via capital gains, and you can earn income from your property. Capital gains refers to the increase in the property's price over time. Historically, the American real estate market has returned 8% over the past 100 years. I'll discuss the specifics of the real estate market later in this chapter.

For now, keep in mind that this 8% is a national figure. There are local pockets of real estate that have done far better than this figure. This is a plus when it comes to real estate, the market moves in a different cycle than the one the stock market moves in.

Real estate gives you ownership of something physical, and this is a huge advantage when one evaluates worst-case scenarios. By having something physical, you can diversify your wealth a lot better. This is something that stocks don't offer.

There are different kinds of real estate properties:

1. Residential
    a. Single family
    b. multi-family
    c. Condos
2. Commercial real estate
    a. Office buildings
    b. Retail space
    c. Shopping centers
3. Industrial

        a. Warehouses
        b. Factories
        c. Power plants
    4. Raw land
        a. Farm land
        b. Timber land/ other land used to grow trees
        c. Ranches
        d. Other use

Let's dive in and take a deeper look at these.

Residential Real Estate

The residential market is the most active for real estate in America. Traditionally, this has been the market that has always received the greatest benefits from the government. One of the reasons for the activity in this market is the constant demand for housing. People will always need a place to live and this ensures constant demand for residential real estate. The most common form of residential real estate is single family housing.

Single Family Homes

As the name suggests, these properties are meant for a single family to live in. The typical home in the suburbs is a single family home. These types of properties provide a steady cash flow to the owner when they're rented because families that occupy a home tend to live there for quite a long time.

Single family homes are also the preferred type of property for lenders to finance, they are usually owner occupied, and the banks know that the borrower has a vested interest in repaying the loan to keep a roof over their heads.

This doesn't mean that it's impossible to qualify for a non-owner occupied property. It's just that the terms you receive might be different and less favorable. A lot depends on your credit score and financial situation. As far as the government is concerned, it would rather finance owner occupied homes. The Federal Housing

Association (FHA) finances properties that are exclusively owner occupied.

The FHA offers a ton of benefits to its applicants as you'll learn later in this chapter.

Multi-Family

A multi-family unit is one that has multiple living units within it. Think of a small block of four apartments or even a tower of apartments. These are quite common in the densely populated areas of the United States, such as near the coasts.

Multi-family units lend themselves very well to certain investment strategies such as house hacking. This is where the owner lives in one unit and places the others on rent thereby reducing their mortgage payment. Multi-family units offer greater amounts of cash flow, and offer the investor a chance to diversify their source of income.

However, they are riskier in that you'll need to deal with multiple tenants. You'll also have to spend more on the maintenance of the property. Usually, landlords choose to hire a manager to do this task but this is something that requires a larger portfolio of properties.

I'll discuss how you can make such an investment truly passive later in this book.

Condos

To the uninitiated, condos and apartments are the same thing. However, to real estate folks, condos are apartments that are managed by a resident's association. Typically, apartment complexes are managed by a company affiliated with a larger real estate investment trust.

Condos can be great investments, but a lot depends on the quality of the property as well as the location. Investors who buy such properties typically target young, working professionals or young, professional couples living in a major city or near one. Some owners invest in condos and use them as vacation rentals. This is especially the case in major cities and tourist areas, such as Hawaii or San Francisco.

The bottom line is that residential real estate is easily accessible for most individuals and, while it costs a decent amount of money, it still represents the cheapest way to get started with real estate investing.

Commercial Real Estate

Commercial real estate tends to be a lot more expensive and usually fluctuates on a different cycle than residential real estate. This provides real estate investors with a good opportunity to diversify their portfolios. However, it can be tough for an individual without prior investment knowledge to access such properties.

Because there is a huge business angle to commercial property, banks will scrutinize the income producing ability of the property as well as your own expertise when it comes to running it. This makes financing tough to acquire.

There are different kinds of commercial property just like there are different kinds of residential real estate properties.

Office Buildings

Office buildings tend to be boom or bust investment vehicles. A good tenant will typically remain for years on end. However, a vacant property takes time to fill. In addition, there are different codes that office buildings will need to satisfy. Since it is a workplace, there are local zoning laws that prescribe safety features that need to be both inspected and maintained regularly.

Violating any of these codes can lead to a large fine and legal headaches for the owner. Usually, large office buildings are managed by companies who have an entire portfolio of them. It is rare for an individual investor to own space like this unless it has been converted from some other type of property.

Retail Space

Retail space is an extremely lucrative investment since many retailers are willing to pay a fixed payment per month along with a share of their overall revenues. This is standard practice in the industry, and it provides landlords with a stake in the business' success.

Having said that, it also exposes the landlord to a large number of safety and regulatory hurdles that can be tough to keep up with. Since customers will be using the space, you will need to ensure that all hazards such as fire and insulation are up to scratch.

Any accidents that occur within your property could leave you exposed to a potential lawsuit. For all of these reasons, banks aren't keen on financing such investments to individuals who lack the expertise or experience when it comes to managing such businesses.

Shopping Centers

A step up from individual retail spaces are shopping centers. As you can imagine these are more expensive to purchase and finance. Thanks to real estate prices being far higher in urban communities, individual investors typically invest in these in more rural areas. In many cases, a company typically owns the property. This doesn't mean you can't invest in shopping centers, though. As you'll learn later in this book, all commercial real estate investment is accessible to you at a fraction of the cost.

Industrial Real Estate

Individuals typically do not invest in such properties. Industrial real estate is usually owned directly by the company that uses it. Even if they do lease space, companies prefer to own their warehouses and other property. After all, these structures are assets that make their way onto their balance sheets.

While physical investment might be out of bounds for the average individual, there are alternative methods to gain exposure to such opportunities. I must mention that storage facilities tend to be classified as either industrial or commercial real estate. These are fully accessible for new investors and are lucrative when done right.

A storage facility is pretty much what it sounds like. You buy a facility that provides storage options such as lockers or units for people to rent. You must be careful when investing in these units. For starters, many beginners tend to buy individual units in a larger facility. For example, if the facility has 100 units, these people buy two or three. Such an investment is a losing proposition. The owner of the facility is probably looking to increase their cash flow from units that are underperforming. As a result, they sell them to you to earn some cash flow. Usually, such purchases are seller financed. You'll learn more about this later in this chapter.

It essentially means that the seller is the one who's extending you a loan, not a bank. When the time comes to rent your facilities out, versus the other owner-owned 97 units, which ones do you think will receive a priority?

As a result of this, the best purchase tends to be one where you buy the entire facility. You're not buying real estate as much as you're buying a business. You'll need to ensure your units are properly secured and that no nefarious activity is going on. You'll have to take care of advertising and reduce your vacancy rates.

It certainly is a full-time job! It's not possible to make this kind of investment passive. However, there are options that are available through the stock market where you can gain exposure to this type of asset. The next chapter will make this clear.

For now, I'll end this section by saying that industrial real estate is a bit inaccessible in the traditional sense for the average investor.

Raw Land

From an inaccessible form of real estate investment, we arrive at one of the most accessible forms. Investing in land used for farming or for growing trees to be used in industry has long been an extremely lucrative way of making money. The best part of such investment is that it is completely passive when done right.

Let's begin with farmland. The United States has the most fertile agricultural land on the planet (The Fertility of North American Soils, 2020). In fact, the Americas occupy three of the top five spots in the world, with Argentina and Uruguay coming in at second and fifth.

U.S. farmland prices also happen to be commensurately higher than the rest of the world. After all, that fertile soil comes at a price. The agricultural sector is dominated by landowning farmers and other corporations that either own the land and lease it out or food manufacturing companies.

As a result, the average investor is stuck buying small parcels of land that might not be the most fertile. However, this is hardly a reason to not invest. Even a relatively less fertile plot of land will yield you a good amount of money once the crops on it are sold. The way it works is that the investor buys the land and leases it to a farmer.

Usually, the farmer who owns plots adjacent to your land is the one who'll lease it. This allows them to extend their natural crop circle, and you as an investor can rest assured that someone knowledgeable is taking care of your land. There are two ways of earning rent.

The first is to ask for a monthly rental payment that is fixed. The second is to ask for a minimum payment and the rest as a proportion of the sales proceeds from the harvest. The former usually yields around three to five percent on your investment, while the latter yields between five and eight percent.

This is over and above the capital gains from the land itself. Land is scarce, and while the value of property that is built on it will rise or fall, the land's value itself will rise over time. It won't rise at the same rate as a building on it. However, you're guaranteed the knowledge that it won't fall.

It isn't as if huge tracts of land are being excavated from the ocean to generate more supply after all!

The other type of raw land investment has to do with growing trees on it for industrial use. Timber, Walnut and Christmas trees offer the investor a lucrative yield. The downside is that trees don't grow overnight. You'll have to wait for five years at the very least for them to grow into a harvestable height.

In the United States, laws govern the sustainability of the trees that are grown for industrial use. As such, you don't need to worry about chopping down rare trees or doing damage to the environment. Walnut is the preferred wood of choice for a lot of furniture, while the other two trees mentioned are self-explanatory in terms of use.

Both of these investment types are completely passive. In the former case, the farmer does all the work. In the latter case, the trees grow on their own schedule and you can hire companies to help you harvest them. In most cases, the buyers of wood will arrange for the collection themselves and all you need to do is collect the check.

Raw land can also be built on to create a ranch or a farm of your choice. Owning land directly means you'll always have a portion of the earth to yourself. This is far more secure than even owning a house.

There are a few smaller categories of land investing wherein investors purchase properties such as mines and mineral rights, in the case of oil, for example. These are not passive by any means and involve significant business risk, so I won't be covering these methods in this book.

The Real Estate Market

There have been many estimates that seek to put a number on the real rate of return of America's housing market. While the exact numbers fluctuate, everyone seems to agree that the figure of 5.5% roughly indicates the real rate of return over the past century (Frankel, 2019).

Keep in mind that this number is heavily affected by the housing market crash of 2007-2008 when property values were destroyed overnight. Prior to the crash, the returns the housing market provided were over eight percent. This is equal to the rate of return the stock market has provided historically.

The thing about real estate is that, to a huge extent, local factors affect prices. For this reason, looking at national numbers doesn't always make sense. The national housing market might be collapsing but the local market in Bemidji, WI might be doing great.

The following factors affect the prices of local real estate:

- Population change
- Rate of demand
- Rate of supply
- Quality of life
- Transaction costs
- Location

Population Change

This factor has to do with how many people are living in the area, as well as how the population number has been changing. For example, if a town is fully dependent on a factory, and if that factory is doing well, population numbers will rise.

However, if that factory is sold or hits hard times, the numbers will plummet. This will lead to less demand for housing, and property values will accordingly fall. This applies to both residential and commercial real estate. Raw land is exempt from these gyrations, mainly because its supply is fixed and it's viewed differently from physical property.

As an investor you should study the population demographics carefully. Investing in an area that is heavily dependent on one or two factors is a bad move that will increase the risk of your investment.

Rate of Demand

This is tied closely to the population change over time. The more people there are in an area, the higher the demand is going to be. Of course, there are other factors that affect demand as well. For example, if the properties are located in an area that isn't desirable, or if they don't offer a good quality of life, people will likely not move there.

The division between renters versus owners is also key to look at. Investing in areas that are primarily owner-occupied leads to more stable property prices since homes are not being sold on the market or advertised for rent very often. This is a secondary factor, but a constant stream of rental listings tends to cause property prices to fluctuate a bit more than usual.

Rate of Supply

If you happen to invest in an area that is constantly experiencing an influx of new homes being built, then you can expect the value of your property to decrease, assuming demand stays the same. This doesn't apply to investments in areas that are still booming.

If your property is among the first to be constructed and is followed by a larger development, then your property's value will rise. However, buying in a mature area that is experiencing oversupply will depress the price of your investment.

Quality of Life

This is the biggest factor that affects the value of your investment. How good are the schools in the area? What is the crime rate? How many employers are present in the area? Are there good entertainment options? Do these options fit the demographic of people living there?

Such factors play a huge role in determining property prices. In fact, zip codes are sometimes changed during the redevelopment of a neighborhood, to imply that it is now part of a more prosperous locality than a run down one. American inner cities often experience such reorganization.

These quality-of-life factors are why the average investor is best served investing in their local area if they choose to go down the physical property route. Since you'll be owning the property itself, it's best to keep an eye on it. Furthermore, you'll be able to quickly figure out the economics of that area and make a better investment choice.

Transaction Costs

As much as property investors wish it, purchase of physical real estate doesn't occur solely between the buyer and the seller. There is an entire industry that is involved in the process, and they need to get paid. From your realtor, to the title agent, to the lawyer responsible for crafting the agreement, everyone has their fees and, the buyer is the one that foots the bill most of the time.

These costs come under the bracket of closing costs and can run you between three and six percent of the property's value. Many investors neglect to budget for this, and as a result, face a shortfall of cash.

Transaction costs in real estate have always been stable. However, a change in the national economic picture can shift these costs higher or lower. For example, mortgage rates depend on the interest rate that the U.S. Federal Bank sets. If rates fall, you can expect a rush to buy new property and to have mortgages refinanced. The opposite happens when rates rise.

Location

Also called 'location, location, location' by real estate developers, this is an important factor for commercial real estate investment. It is composed of all the factors listed above and a few intangibles. With regards to residential real estate, this doesn't play as huge a factor since there will always be demand for housing.

With commercial real estate this isn't the case. For example, if a company is looking for office space and are presented with two adjacent buildings, they're going to pick the one that fits their brand better. As a result, location plays a very important role. It's unlikely that some hot, tech startup is going to lease space on the wrong side of the tracks in Palo Alto.

When investing in commercial properties, you should pay special attention to this since it is a bigger portion of the picture than it is with residential properties.

The Advantages of Real Estate Investment Over Other Options

Real estate is often talked about as being one of the best modes of investment. Why exactly is this? The best way to figure this out is to look at the alternatives. For scalability and convenience, the stock market is the only option that is comparable. It should come as no surprise that these two avenues of investment are often compared to one another.

Let's look at the advantages that real estate provides the investor when compared to the stock market.

Economic Cycle

One of the biggest disadvantages of investing in stocks is that all of them are subject to broad economic cycles. The economy depends on a ton of macroeconomic factors that can't always be predicted or even understood. For example, few people saw the dotcom crash coming in the year 2000.

The stock markets are vulnerable to all kinds of risks. An unexpected event sends stocks tumbling and your investment with it. This is not the case with real estate. As I've explained already, real estate values tend to depend a lot more on local economics than national or global factors.

If stocks are tumbling, or if unemployment is high, the national numbers will look bad. However, the factors of primary importance for the value of your property are the ones mentioned in the previous section. How is the population growth? What is the quality of life? And so on.

These factors cause the real estate portion of your portfolio to perform at a different pace to your stock market portion. It allows you to diversify better, and your properties will act as a hedge against stock market downturns. It also allows you to stay ahead of the curve since you'll have a better handle on local economics than the national picture. This allows you to adjust your investment accordingly.

Inflation

Inflation is a result of natural economics. Prices of goods in an economy keep rising over time if everything goes well. This is because as the economy expands, more money is created. The increased supply of money means that the prices of goods and services keep pace with this increase.

As long as inflation keeps pace with the growth of the economy, things are great. The problem occurs when inflation outpaces the latter, resulting in people having less money and everything getting more expensive. This leads to economic meltdowns of the kind Venezuela and Zimbabwe have experienced in recent times.

The stock market does not protect you from inflation. It isn't guaranteed to rise at a rate greater than inflation does over the long term. This is because you're investing in businesses that can prosper or fall depending on what the economy is like. In contrast, real estate values (residential) tend to keep pace with inflation. While they might fall, when a crisis of the sort seen in 2008 occurs, they will typically rebound and keep pace with inflation. Since everyone needs a home, residential real estate is a necessary product. Therefore, its price will keep pace with the value of money in an economy.

The 'value of money' is nothing but inflation. Thus, by investing in property, you're assured of the fact that the value of your money, or its purchasing power, doesn't decrease over time, at the very least.

Physical Ownership

Another massive advantage of real estate investment is that you own something physical and tangible. A stock portfolio, no matter how huge, is still a bunch of numbers. It isn't something you can point to and claim as yours. Sure, you own a chunk of profitable businesses by investing in stocks, but it's unlikely that the management of those companies will call you and ask for your input.

You can't change the direction of the company through your decisions. All you have is a vote, and even that is heavily diluted. In contrast, if you want to change the roof of your house to neon green, you're free to do so. If something goes wrong, you always have a physical space to shelter you.

This provides people with a huge sense of security and peace of mind. This is something that you should take into consideration when investing your money. Some people value it less than others, but everyone desires it to a certain extent. Real estate provides a great way to gain this peace of mind.

Cash Flow

If you invest in rental properties, real estate gives you a great way to mobilize your investment in two ways. Not only are you earning money through capital gains, you're also receiving cash returns on your investment. You can achieve this through stock market investments as well, but it isn't possible with every single stock purchase.

Some stocks pay dividends but it isn't compulsory for companies to do this. What's more, the yield on these dividends is usually around two to three percent. Rental yields in properties vary depending on the location, but it isn't impossible to earn close to five percent yields on your investment.

If you manage to buy a property at below market price and improve its condition, you could earn as much as seven to eight percent on your investment. This means the amount of cash you receive monthly is going to be a lot higher when compared to stock investments.

You can use this cash to reinvest in the property or for some other investment. Your money therefore grows faster.

These are the biggest advantages of real estate investment when compared to investing in stocks. As great as they are, there are some disadvantages as well. Let's look at these now.

Disadvantages of Real Estate Versus Other Investments

While real estate investment gives you ownership of physical property, it turns out that this can be a disadvantage as well, depending on your personal situation

Illiquidity

Liquidity refers to how easily an asset can be bought or sold. Stocks and investments in them can be bought and sold at the click of a button. So, your money is always available to you to be put to work on any other investment opportunity you might have going on.

This isn't the case with real estate. Let's say you have $10,000 in stocks versus $10,000 in equity built up in your property. The former is effectively cash since it can be sold and you'll have that money in your account within a day. The equity that is built in your property cannot be cashed out so easily.

You'll have to refinance the property and hope that the new appraisal of the property leads to terms that allows you to cash out that amount of money from it. It's a lengthy process that takes around a month from start to receiving the money in your bank account.

The other disadvantage, in terms of illiquidity, is that it takes time to sell a property. Most properties remain on the market for around a month or even more in the case of expensive properties. Combine a down, property market, and you could witness a property that is up for sale for over a year.

The longer your property remains on the market, the more its value decreases since buyers will figure out that you're not receiving the price you want. All of this makes exiting a property investment a bit tough.

Leverage

Leverage refers to powering your investment with debt. When you buy a property using a mortgage, you're signing up for half a lifetime's worth of debt payments. This isn't the case with stock investments. While the impact of mortgage payments can be reduced greatly by rental income, it is possible to do the math wrong or to even use a mortgage incorrectly.

For example, a lot of people draw a mortgage and then live in their own homes. This means they need to pay the full mortgage amount to the bank for the term of the loan, and they don't have cash coming in from the property. They're solely reliant on capital gains appreciation.

As you've already learned, cashing in capital gains from properties is a lengthy process. All of this makes it very important for you to understand what a mortgage really is, and to prioritize cash flow from your real estate property to reduce the debt burden. Don't do this, and you'll easily turn a potential asset into a liability.

Active Income

The Internal Revenue Service (IRS) classifies rental income as being passive, but truth be told, it's very hard to classify it this way in real life. Managing tenants and their shenanigans is hard. Some of them won't pay on time, some of them will damage your property, you'll need to follow local ordinances when closing lease deals, etc.

In some cases, you might even be liable for any injury a tenant sustains. Being a landlord has many benefits, but it has its drawbacks as well. Before investing in rental property you need to build a passive framework around it and account for how much this will cost you.

This disadvantage can be mitigated by investing in the options I've highlighted in this book. Just keep in mind that physical real estate isn't all about the advantages. Like with everything else, there are some negatives.

Transaction Costs

I've mentioned these already. Real estate purchases involve high transaction costs that amount to as much as six percent of the overall value of the property. This is a huge sum when you're talking about properties that are over $100,000 in value.

Add to this the initial investment of between 10-20% of the property as down payment, and you have a high barrier of entry. This isn't the case with stocks and you can get started with as little as $100. Most brokers offer zero commissions these days and it costs you nothing to invest in the market.

More Work

The stock market has an easy solution for you to invest in it without putting much thought into your choices. They're called index funds and exchange traded funds (ETFs). These two types of funds simply track broad stock market indices, and you'll find that, with a simple purchase, you'll gain exposure to the entire world of stocks.

This is not the case with real estate, especially physical real estate. You'll need to evaluate all of the factors I discussed earlier and will have to put in the work. If you choose to adopt investment strategies such as rehabbing and flipping homes, your time spent on the property increases exponentially.

This makes it difficult for the average person to invest in real estate in a sustainable manner.

Appreciation Isn't Guaranteed

Technically, nothing is guaranteed to appreciate forever, so this isn't so much a disadvantage of real estate as much as it has to do with investment as a whole. Many people invest in real estate, thanks to hearing myths about how property prices always appreciate and so on.

This is what caused the housing market crash in 2007-2008. Property values do rise at the rate of inflation, but this doesn't mean investing in them is a sure thing. Always do your homework before investing your money in everything. Real estate is no exception.

Traditional Real Estate Strategies

It's now time to look briefly at a few methods that real estate investors use to make money in properties. All of these involve physical real estate investment and require the use of leverage. Of course, you can buy properties for cash as well, if you have access to that much money.

Most people don't, and this is why leverage or financing is a constant theme of real estate investment. Let's take a deeper look at this to understand how it works.

Financing

A mortgage is simply a home loan rebranded. You'll have to make payments over the term of the loan, and will need to place a down payment, as well as closing costs, before you can take ownership of the property. The down payment reflects your ownership or equity in the property.

There are two kinds of loans that are offered by lenders. The first is a mixed loan where your payment results in both the principal and the interest being paid. The second is an interest-only loan where all payments made are towards interest. After a certain period, the lender will require you to pay down the principal as well.

This second type of loan is trouble. It's exactly the same as borrowing money on your credit card and then paying just the minimum balance every month, instead of clearing your entire outstanding balance. That balance remains intact, and you're only generating more debt for yourself.

Interest-only loans are packaged in attractive terms. Sometimes they're called variable-rate loans or adjustable-rate mortgages (ARMs). Then there's the monstrosity called the no-money-down ARM, which allows people to put nothing down, make interest-only payments for a fixed period of time, and then pay the principal as well along with interest, after the initial period ends.

This higher payment is cloaked as being a higher, 'adjusted' interest rate. People who seek such loans don't pay attention to the fine print regarding the adjustment, and risk being foreclosed on when this higher rate hits. If the message isn't already clear, you need to stay away from interest-only loans.

The good news is that in America, more than half of the mortgages on offer are mixed mortgages, meaning you'll pay both principal and interest with your monthly payment. This isn't the case in other developed economies, such as the United Kingdom and Australia, where interest-only loans dominate.

Applying for a mortgage is a lengthy process and requires a lot of paperwork. Since the amount of financing you can qualify for is such an important portion of the purchase process, lenders will pre-qualify you. This allows you to submit income documents to the bank, and they issue you a letter detailing the amount they can lend you and what your payments will be.

This isn't a full approval, but it helps you look at properties that are within your means, instead of negotiating prices with a seller and then finding out you can't finance the property. Lenders use two simple ratios to calculate your creditworthiness. The first is the front ratio.

The front ratio is the mortgage payment divided by your monthly, pre-tax income. Lenders look for this to be less than 24%. If your mortgage payment is $500 and you earn $1,000, this puts your front ratio at 50%, which is double what the average lender looks for.

The second ratio is the back ratio. This is calculated by dividing your existing debt payments and your mortgage payment by your monthly income. Lenders look for this to be less than 36%. If your mortgage payment is $500, your student loan debt is $300 and your car payment is $250, you'll need to have a monthly income of at least $2,916 to qualify.

These ratios are not set in stone. Sometimes, lenders will ignore them if there is a special circumstance such as an inheritance or a high degree of cash savings. The usual documentation such as, your payslips, employment letter and tax returns will have to be submitted.

Once the financing is approved, you search for properties, make an offer, and sign the purchase agreement. Your down payment is transferred to an escrow account, the bank wires the money into escrow, and the escrow agent transfers this money to the seller. The title is transferred to your name and the property is officially yours!

Sources

You will need to source good investment opportunities. Real estate investors frequent local investing clubs in their area to source leads and to also network with other professionals in the industry who can help them out with certain tasks. If you plan on being a landlord, it's a good idea to meet these people if you want to find a handyman or a contractor who can help you with your property.

There are many websites, such as Zillow and Roofstock, that help you source deals. I'll discuss these in more detail later in the book. You can also scour the neighborhood and look at classifieds for sale listings.

Your local realtor is the best source of properties. By letting them know that you're in the market for a certain type of property, they'll be able to source relevant listings for you. They do this by accessing the Multiple Listing System or MLS. An MLS is typically owned by an association of realtors, and this is where the most recent and up-to-date property listings are found.

You need to be a real estate professional in order to get access to the MLS. Sites such as Zillow don't provide access to it through their listings. The biggest advantage of the MLS is that it allows you to view all the relevant data of properties sold in the area. This is useful when preparing comps or comparables.

A comp is a study of properties similar to the one you're looking to buy to determine an appropriate selling price. It's an important part of the process since you'll need to do this to figure out what to offer to a seller.

Let's now take a look at the first investment strategy.

Turnkey Rentals

This is the most common method of investing in real estate. Turnkey refers to properties that are ready to rent and don't require any repairs or improvements. More often than not they already have tenants within them, and as an investor, you'll earn cash flow from the first day.

There are advantages to this model. Immediate cash flow is the primary one. There's also the fact that by having tenants in the place, you don't have to worry too much about managing the property beyond doing what the previous landlord has done. You'll be able to get a feel for the work required, immediately.

Since tenants are present, you'll also be able to analyze the profitability of the property using real numbers, and won't have to project anything. In turn, agents and other professionals will be able to give you extremely accurate prices for the property since everything is stable.

Turnkey rentals are the easiest investment to make passive. I'll discuss how to do this later in this book.

The disadvantage of turnkey rentals is that you're not going to receive a bargain on the price. Given that the property has so many things going for it, you'll pay market prices, or even a small premium, to purchase the property. It's best suited for investors who want to earn steady cash flow and aren't too worried about earning outsized capital gains.

House Hacking

This is perhaps the best way to finance an owner-occupied property. Many people utilize this method to own property, live in it, and reduce their debt burden every month. The way it works is that a person finances a multi-family unit and occupies one of the units.

They collect rent from the other units and use this money to reduce their mortgage payments. House hacking can be implemented by utilizing FHA mortgages, which greatly reduces the down-payment requirements. FHA loans require the property in question to be owner-occupied, and this removes other investment strategies from contention.

Since you'll be occupying one of the units in your property, it is considered owner-occupied. Over time, you'll have more of your monthly cash flow to devote to other investments, or you could pay your loan principal down faster. In some cases, the rental payment is greater than the mortgage payment.

In effect, such owners get paid to own property which is a massive win.

Flipping

Most beginners to real estate think of flipping homes, when someone mentions real estate investment. This involves locating a property that is rundown and needs repairs. The investor puts money into rehabbing the place and then sells it for a higher price. It is a profitable way of investing money indeed.

There are a few downsides to this you must be aware of. First, it isn't a passive source of income at all. You'll need to intimately know the neighborhood and constantly be on the lookout for great deals. If your realtor is bringing you deals, then it's probably too late and you're too far down the chain.

This is because the competition is high, and the experienced flippers source deals directly from the

MLS. In some cases, flippers place offers within a few hours of the listing going live! They're experienced enough to gauge their costs and returns by just looking at the photos and making a few phone calls.

This sets a high barrier for the beginner investor to overcome. As a result, it's best for novice investors to start with house hacking or turnkey rental investing, before becoming a rehabber. You will need deep contacts in the industry to help you lower your rehab costs and to make your offer quickly.

Many rehabbers use a method called cash-out refinancing to withdraw their profits from the property and to invest it into another property. This is a bit complicated and isn't in the scope of this book. Since it isn't a passive way of investment, it doesn't make sense to delve into how this works.

Buy, Rehab, Rent, Refinance, Repeat

Also called BRRRR, this is a strategy that combines the power of rental investment with flipping. It begins as a flipping strategy. The investor seeks out properties requiring rehabilitation, and they fix them. Once the property is spruced up, they rent it out to people and earn rental income on them, thereby reducing their debt burden.

After enough equity is built up in the property, they refinance the property using the cash-out refinance method and invest their cash into another property. In this manner, they build a portfolio of properties that give them steady cash flow every month, and they get to enjoy the boost in capital gains they've received as well.

As with rehabbing this is not a passive strategy.

So how can you invest in real estate passively and with less money? There are a number of options for you to do this. Some of them are more recent than others. For the rest of this book, I'll be focusing on how to turn your real estate investing completely passive.

Chapter 2:

Essential Things to Know

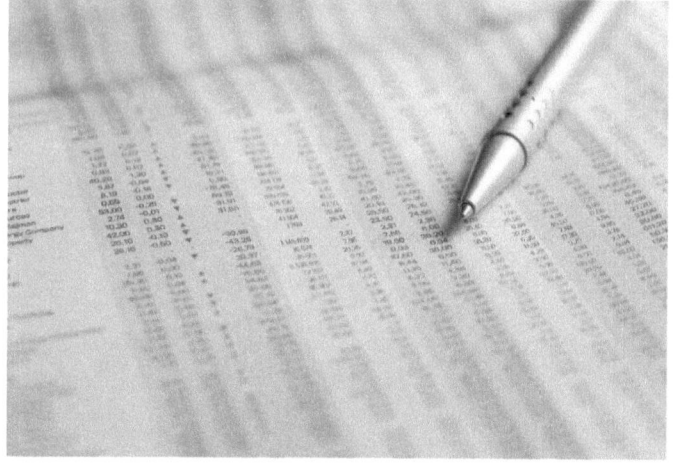

Before jumping into any real estate investment, you should do your homework. This is easy enough to say, but what constitutes homework exactly? This is the focus of this chapter. All real estate opportunities, whether passive or active, revolve around a few basic terms and concepts. By aligning yourself with these, you'll be able to ensure that the odds of a successful investment will be high.

One of the first things to keep in mind is that risk is ever present. Some investors seek opportunities that have no risk attached to them, they spend their days looking for sure things. The result is that they keep looking for the rest of their lives while their money gets eaten up by inflation thanks to it remaining on the sidelines. Here's the thing: Risk is always going to be present in any deal you undertake. What matters is how well you mitigate those risks.

Risk is a very personal thing. What I mean is, the perception of risk is different between different people. A person who makes $10,000 per month is going to view a $400,000 investment very differently from someone who makes this amount in six months. The first step to figuring out risk, is to look at your own profile and see whether you are willing to have your financial status take a hit.

For starters, do you have enough money saved up to pay for at least three months' living expenses? This is crucial to have since it ensures you have enough cushion in case things go wrong. Remember, if you're planning on assuming a mortgage, this amount will need to be saved up as well, or else you'll risk losing your property.

If you default on mortgage payments and go through a foreclosure, you can kiss your credit score goodbye. You won't be able to borrow money for a period of at least three years, so it's crucial that you build adequate backup into all of your living expenses and in your investments.

Next, you'll need to look at how stable your job situation is. If you don't work a regular job, how steady is your cash inflow? Can you rely on it and to what degree? Is there any room in it to pay for a mortgage every month? You might find that despite having saved up enough for a down payment, you don't have enough monthly cash flow to cover mortgage payments.

Some people go ahead anyway and assume the mortgage, since they think they're buying an asset. What they don't realize is that they've just assumed a payment for the next 20 to 30 years that they cannot afford. Therefore, work on increasing your income before you apply for a mortgage, if you can't cover it.

If you have any outstanding debt, it is imperative that you clear it. This isn't just practical sense, it's financial as well. The more debt you have on your record, the worse your financing terms will be. Some of the options listed in this book allow you to invest in real estate without assuming a mortgage.

You can invest in them instead of financing a purchase, if you have debt. The point is to not add to your existing debt mountain. If you do so, you'll only make it more likely that you will be unable to pay off your debt.

Assuming all of these items check out favorably, you're now in a good financial position to assume a mortgage. However, this doesn't necessarily mean that you should.

This is where your psychological profile comes into play. The key to success in real estate investment, is to invest your money for the long term.

You'll need to weather short-term emotional swings in order to do this. Your investment needs time to mature and to grow. Think back to how raw land investing works. The trees and crops on your land will take time to mature, and you can't expect them to rise overnight!

The same applies to investment in real estate. Whether it is traditional investment in any of the strategies listed in the previous chapter, or the ones you're about to learn, you'll have to be impervious to short-term irrationality. This is easier said than done. You might read the news and become convinced that the real estate market is about to crash. You might be tempted to pull all of your money out.

Worse, you might invest your money in some opportunity only to find that the market has crashed completely. This means you've lost 50% of your investment right off the bat. Will you be able to hold on to your investment throughout all of this? Will you stay the course and continue to hold for the long term?

Most people don't, and this is why they find real estate success so hard to come by. If you lack adequate capital to invest in physical real estate, then the situation is even worse. Then, you'll usually be investing via the stock market, and that is a minefield of emotions.

Financial news anchors are either predicting doomsday, or they're predicting the best of times. There's no in between. Before investing into any opportunity, ask yourself:

- Am I willing to watch this decline to half its value? Am I willing to lose that much money on paper?
- Will I still hold on to it? (You need to hold on to it in order to make money.)

In the first question, the term 'on paper' is extremely important. There is a difference between realized and unrealized gains. Realized gains are losses of money. This is money that you cannot recover from this opportunity. It occurs when you fully close out your transaction. The same categorization applies to gains as well. For example, if you buy a property for $100,000, and sell it for $150,000, you've realized a gain of $50,000.

If that property's value rises to $150,000, and if you decide to hang onto it instead of selling it, you now have an unrealized gain of $50,000. These are paper gains and aren't real cash. The same applies to losses. When the stock market declines, you'll hear news anchors make statements like 'investors lost $5 trillion today'.

This is an inaccurate statement. That number only refers to how much the market value of all investments in the market declined by. They could be realized or unrealized. If investors sold that much stock, it becomes realized. If they hold on to it, it's still unrealized, and there is every chance of them recovering those gains.

Another news item that often grabs headlines is when some wealthy person suffers a reduction in their net worth. For example, if Facebook's stock declines, some news outlets publish headlines such as, 'Mark Zuckerberg sees $1 billion wiped off his net worth.'

Again, this is a nonsensical headline that has probably been written by someone who has no idea how money works. That $1 billion that has been 'wiped off' is only on paper. Do you really think Zuckerberg is panicking because his paper worth has reduced? Or do you think he's focused on running his company?

As an investor you need to maintain focus on the fundamentals of your investment. As long as it makes sense, you need to keep purchasing it. If its price declines, and if it's fundamentals are still in place, then you need to buy more. If it was a good buy at $50, then surely, it's an even better buy at $30, right?

Adopt a business mindset to your investments and keep emotion out of it. Don't invest in something just because it looks like your childhood home, or because the name of the street the property's on is the same as your second ex-wife. You're investing to make money, so keep the focus on evaluating its income potential.

Everything else is noise. This will help you reassess risk in a rational way. It'll also keep you invested for the long-term without having to worry about the short-term fluctuations in price.

Location

Let's dive deeper into the various aspects of location and how you need to evaluate it when it comes to your real estate investment. I've already touched upon this in the previous chapter. The fact is that the condition and the sale price of a property can be changed.

You can enhance a property, improve its curbside appeal, and add some features that demand a greater selling price. The only thing you cannot change is its location. You could have the prettiest looking property, but if it's located in a crime infested area, then nothing that you do is going to make a difference.

For the most part, location is also what drives demand. Certain zip codes are a lot more desirable than others and will always experience more demand. This is why redevelopment projects routinely expand or contract zip code boundaries in order to affect the demand and the perceived value of the property.

Here are some of the factors that go into making a great location.

History of Capital Growth

Take a look at the median home values in the area over the course of 50 years or so. Some areas tend to have shorter histories than others, thanks to redevelopment efforts. What you want to look for is a steady upward curve in capital appreciation that is, at least, greater than inflation.

Properties with a stable history of price appreciation will be able to withstand any adverse circumstances that affect their prices in the future. This doesn't mean they won't decline in value, but it does indicate that they might not decline as much, assuming things remain relatively normal in that neighborhood.

Presence of a Hub

In the previous chapter, I mentioned that properties close to just one major source of employment are risky investments, since so much demand is determined by that single source. This begs the question, what sort of an employment profile do you want the neighborhood to have?

In short, you want it to be close to a major hub or city. Suburban properties are highly sought after, since almost all of them are close to a major hub. Hubs tend to have varied sources of employment, and you're not tied to a single factory or even industry.

While some big cities have an overload of one particular industry, they still tend to offer enough employment opportunities to residents. For example, New York City is heavily concentrated in finance, but it's a big enough city to support other industries as well. If a downturn does occur, as it did in 2008, the city's and its suburbs' property values won't plummet as much.

For example, examining the state of property, in the state of New Jersey, since 2006, is instructive (Stirling, 2018). The state saw its property values peak in 2006, right before the devaluation that began in 2007.

As of this writing, large parts of the state have still not recovered anything close to their peak 2006 values. However, this doesn't apply to every single town in the state. New Jersey acts as one big suburb to the major cities of New York and Philadelphia. Uniformly, every town and suburb that is close to rail connections to these cities, or is across the water from them, has witnessed an increase in property values above the 2006 peak.

The cities of Hoboken and Weehawken are the towns whose property values have risen the most since the crisis. It isn't a coincidence that both these towns are right across the water from Manhattan. Towns in the rural areas of Jersey haven't come anywhere close to their pre-crisis levels.

Gentrification

Gentrification refers to the redevelopment of a previously run-down area that leads to an influx of more wealthy residents. It has a large number of critics, since this invariably results in a neighborhood becoming a little to squeaky clean. However, as a property investor, there's a lot to love about it.

Perhaps the biggest examples of gentrification, over the past three decades, are Manhattan and Brooklyn. Large areas of the borough were drug-infested, crime zones but these same areas are now thriving communities. Areas, such as Tompkins Square Park, were notorious for their preponderance of drug related violence, but concerted efforts by the government resulted in that area being enveloped into the larger neighborhood of Alphabet City.

As a result, once the area was ridden of crime, property values rose astronomically. Similar situations played out in Harlem, Bushwick and Williamsburg. Some savvy investors look to invest in neighborhoods that stand a good chance of gentrification, but this is pretty risky for the beginner to try out.

If your plans don't come off, and if the city doesn't push the neighborhood's redevelopment, you're stuck with a property no one wants. It's best to stick to gentrified neighborhoods that attract stable tenants who will ensure you receive good amounts of cash flow.

Crime and Vacancy Rates

What are the two factors that affect the quality of life statistics in a neighborhood more than anything else? The answer is: crime rates and rental vacancy rates. Rental vacancy rates are different from property vacancy rates (or vacants, as they're called.)

Vacants indicate a neighborhood that is dying or is already dead. Those properties are effectively condemned and their owners have given up on them. They'll likely be bought out by the government and made a part of some special scheme. Vacant rentals refer to the number of rental listings you'll find online for a neighborhood.

Look at the quality of accommodation on offer and you'll be able to gauge the kind of tenant existing landlords are targeting. Are they separating larger units into temporary partitions and charging rent? Or are they advertising the entire apartment? Partitioning or subletting usually indicates that people are not able to afford rents in that neighborhood, and that property prices are well beyond the ordinary investors' reach.

Because they are so high, you can't expect them to appreciate too much either. This is the case in cities such as New York and San Francisco, as well as in popular vacation spots like Miami and Hawaii. Property prices are driven, in part, thanks to demand, but there is a limit to the exorbitant rents people can afford.

As a result, landlords need to partition their apartments to smaller units to make living affordable. This decreases the quality of life in some areas and it results in only slightly higher rental yields. If you see a large number of listings in a particular area, it's a pretty good indicator that such properties are not good investments.

Crime is self-explanatory when it comes to the quality of life. Look for declining or low crime rates. Neighborhoods that do not have many properties advertised for rent are good investment bets, since it indicates that people snap them up before they hit the open market.

Entertainment Options and Schools

Stable renters tend to favor a balanced life, and this means the presence of entertainment options close by, along with good schools for their kids. Single-family homes' locations are mostly evaluated on this basis. The presence of a good school nearby will push property prices a lot higher.

Your aim as a landlord should be to attract stable tenants. The higher their quality of life, the better. This way you won't have to worry about your property remaining vacant and not earning any cash flow from it.

Location plays an important role in this and you should seek to find a balance between paying a premium for property prices versus choosing a great location. Central Park West or Beverly Hills are undoubtedly good locations in which to own property. It's just that you'll pay an arm and a leg (and possible the rest of yourself) to buy property there. As a result, you won't earn much of a return on it in terms of cash flow.

Renters to Owners Ratio

This was something I mentioned in the earlier chapter as well. Ideally, you'll buy property in a neighborhood that has a large number of owner-occupied property as opposed to a large number of renters. This brings stability to property prices. Here's why this happens.

A steady stream of rental ads allows the market to appraise the value of property in that neighborhood. Rental yields are relatively stable throughout locations. If you know that the average rental yield of a location is four percent, and if you see a property being advertised for rent for $1,500 per month, you can conclude that the property's value must be roughly (1500*12/0.04) $450,000.

Such appraisals will lead to buyers looking at the neighborhood more often and making offers on properties there. As property sales happen, the official prices of the neighborhood will fluctuate a lot more, thanks to the steady stream of comps being generated.

When you decide to sell your property, you'll find that you'll face much tougher negotiations and will not receive the price you're looking for. The buyer just has so much more data to work with. I don't mean to say that you'll make a loss. My point is that you want fluctuations to remain low so you can get a better deal when you sell.

Owner-occupied properties also ensure that the demographics of the neighborhood remain the same over long periods of time. A large number of rental properties means that the people living there are transient, and who knows what the makeup of the neighborhood might be a few years from now?

This builds additional instability into prices, a quality you want to avoid.

Factors That Reduce Property Values

There are a range of factors, other than the ones mentioned above, that work to reduce the value of property. Watch out for the presence or development of these with any prospective investment.

Pollution or Noise

People want to live in desirable areas that provide a high quality of life. Pollution and incessant noise figure nowhere in this equation. The presence of factories or a power plant tend to make renters squeamish about living in the neighborhoods near them.

More often than not, concerns about groundwater pollution tend to affect communities near industrial plants. Despite the strict environmental regulation surrounding these plants, some pollution does occur. Factories also result in elevated noise levels, thanks to the large volume of work that is carried out within them.

The presence of railroad crossings or tracks near residential properties tend to reduce property values as well. Rail traffic at odd hours of the night does tons of damage to property value, and you'll find that no one will want to rent such places.

Once you own a property, watch out for such developments or plans. In such situations, it can be tough to decide what to do. Often selling the property before things get worse might be the best option. These days, there is a new concern when it comes to industrial installations.

The presence of 5G towers has attracted a lot of debate around the world, with some people even resorting to burning them to the ground. While the authorities claim that these towers pose no health risk to those nearby, it can be tough for the general public to get on board with this message.

Watch for the presence of these towers close to your property.

Rezoning

Rezoning usually means good things as far as property owners are concerned, but every once in a while, the boundaries are redrawn and a few unlucky owners end up on the wrong side of the new boundaries. In the United States, zoning laws play a huge role when it comes to property values.

This is because such laws prescribe the kinds of businesses that can operate in certain areas. For example, liquor stores and gun stores are prohibited from operating within a certain distance from school zones. The frustrating thing for the property investor is that different states apply these laws differently.

This makes it imperative that you conduct your research thoroughly before deciding to invest. Pay special attention to any governmental chatter about how zoning is conducted and whether city officials are planning on rezoning any areas of the city.

The reclassification of a residential zone to a mixed use zone might result in a number of businesses popping up that are undesirable, and that might reduce the quality of life in the neighborhood. Investors need to be constantly aware of such plans and their implications for property prices.

This doesn't mean you need to remain awake at night worrying about this. Instead, look at the history of the municipality or county and examine how often lines have been redrawn. Places that have a history of doing this tend to follow this example in the future. You might want to consider a more stable place to invest if this is the case.

Foreclosures and Short Sales

A short sale occurs when a property owner sells their investment for less than the amount that is due on their mortgage (Chen, 2020). This often happens when the seller is underwater on their mortgage.

Underwater, or upside down as it's sometimes called, refers to the property being worth less than the outstanding amount on the mortgage. This, along with foreclosures, cause property prices to tumble massively in the neighborhood. A single foreclosure is unlikely to pull property prices down all by itself. However, a raft of them will result in all property values becoming depressed. This happens because the market will assume that some common factor affecting everyone in that neighborhood is causing foreclosures. Neighborhoods that depend on a single source of employment, such as a nearby factory, suffer from this malaise.

If the factory shuts down, foreclosures soon follow and property values are wiped out. While short sales still allow the sellers to escape a foreclosure, this is hardly a good state to be in. Most lenders don't allow owners to sell their homes. Remember that as long as a mortgage is in place, the buyer doesn't fully own the property.

Therefore, any sale has to be ratified with the bank or lender. Banks in turn allow short sales only if they determine that there is no way they can ever recover the mortgage value, and are willing to write off the loan and recover whatever they can. Thus, a short sale is even worse for property prices than a single foreclosure is.

A single foreclosure might have been driven by some misfortune native to the seller. However, a short sale involves the expert opinion of the bank, and if they approve of it, it indicates that property prices are probably overvalued and that they handed out a bad loan.

You can check with local realtors for history of foreclosures and short sales. Watch out for a high frequency of them. Generally, screening for neighborhoods that have high owner-occupied properties will keep you well away from this issue. If people still own property and live in the neighborhood, then there's less possibility of a history of foreclosures.

Power Lines

This is a highly controversial topic. According to research cited by Forbes, there is no definitive scientific basis by which magnetic fields generated by high voltage power lines can ever cause cancer (Salzberg, 2014). However, there is also enough evidence of the presence of cancer clusters in communities near high voltage power lines to suggest that such cases are not a coincidence.

Leaving health concerns aside, what does this mean for property prices? It should be fairly obvious. Neighborhoods near power lines are considered highly undesirable and you'll end up attracting a transient sort of tenant. No matter how great the property is, or how nicely trimmed the landscape is, you're not going to convince a family with children to move in there.

This means you'll likely be faced with a situation where you'll have to constantly advertise the property as being available for rent, as will the other owners in the neighborhood. This is a hallmark of an area that is undesirable to own property in, and you'll struggle to exit your investment.

It's best to simply stay away from such investment opportunities to begin with.

Gun Ranges and Sex Offenders

The reason most gun ranges are located far away from nearby residential communities, is because of the safety concerns that result in property values getting depressed. Another demographic factor that depresses property values is the presence of registered sex offenders in the area.

Safety issues are at the top of the heap when it comes to quality of life. Most investors consider the crime rate and leave it at that, but these particular issues can cause property prices to come tumbling down as well.

Highways

Highways tend to bring pollution and noise to a neighborhood. Another factor, closely related to highways, is the presence of an overhead flight path. As planes land, there will be not just noise, but also vibration that ends up ruining the quality of life of people living underneath it.

If your property is on a flight path and is close enough to the airport, leasing it to a hotel operator will make a lot of sense. However, proximity is important in this case. You can consider such properties around airports or travel hubs. However, if the property is far from any major travel hub, such as a railway, bus station or airport, you're best off staying away.

If a highway or major thoroughfare springs up overnight, you can consider enhancing the property's soundproofing. This will allow you to charge slightly higher rents since your tenants will appreciate the additional effort. It can be a good way to differentiate your property from the other nearby. Also keep in mind that the creation of a transport hub near your property results in values increasing. So it isn't a fully negative situation. A lot depends on the property and neighborhood in question.

If you spot such properties online do not purchase them until you're visited them in person. If you can see yourself living there, then your tenants will as well. If not, move on and find something else.

Curb Appeal

Curb appeal is an all-encompassing item that takes into account that property's exterior, the conditions of the landscaping, as well as the state of the homes in the neighborhood. You can have the best-looking property, but if every property around yours looks terrible, there's nothing you can do to increase property value.

Keep this point in mind when making enhancements to your property as well. For example, you might want to build the property up some more to increase its value. However, if the rest of the neighborhood doesn't keep up, you're probably not going to attract the prices you want.

Remember to consider all of these factors before you purchase a property in any form. It'll save you a ton of headaches down the road.

Important Numbers to be Aware Of

This section will introduce you to all of the key numbers to be aware of when investing in real estate. Some of them need to be monitored after a purchase, while some of them will play a major role in determining whether you should invest or not.

Median Listing Price

How do you know whether the price you're being asked to pay is justified or not? Compare it to the median listing price. This is the average price of a property being sold in that area. Keep in mind that the median is the average price of all properties, not just the type of property you're looking at. If you're looking at purchasing a two bedroom unit, but the majority of listings in the neighborhood are of three bedroom units, the sale price of your unit is going to be lower than the median. You'll need to adjust it to reflect the condition of your property.

This is where a good realtor comes in handy. You should check with them with regards to how they prepare their comps and have them walk you through the process. The preparation of a comp begins with finding nearby, comparable property sales to yours, and working backwards from there to adjust for the current property's condition.

Errors can creep into the process if there are no comparable sales in the nearby area. This means the realtor has to search a wider zone and that may remove them from the demographics of the current neighborhood. Thus, there is some art to the process. By having them explain it to you, you can judge for yourself whether what they're telling you makes sense or not.

Occupancy Rate

This is calculated by dividing the amount of square feet occupied in a neighborhood by the total available space. In other words, how much of the neighborhood is vacant compared to occupied. A 100% occupancy rate is desirable, although this won't often be the case. It's tough to put a firm number on a desirable occupancy rate since so much depends on the type of property as well as the neighborhood.

It's best to take a tour of the neighborhood before purchasing anything in it. If you're investing through a vehicle, as I'll illustrate in the next chapter, you should verify that the management knows what they're doing in this regard.

As long as you don't see too many vacant signs or to let signs, you'll be fine.

Net Income or Net Operating Income

NOI, as it's often called, is the measure of profit you earn from the property. It is calculated by subtracting the expenses of running the property (maintenance, vacancy, utilities if any) from the rent received.

It's a figure that should be monitored both before and after purchasing a property. You might be wondering how you can possibly estimate expenses prior to purchasing a property? Well, this is where a handy rule of thumb comes into play.

The 50% rule in real estate states that your expenses will usually be half of the rent that you collect. If you collect $1,000 per month in rents, your expenses should be budgeted at $500. This means you can expect to collect 50% of rent as profit and this is your NOI.

This is a rough figure, but it works out more often than not. Some investors apply another rule before the 50% called the one percent rule. This states that the monthly income earned from a property must be at least one percent of the purchase price. If the property is selling for $100,000, it must earn at least $1,000 in rent every month.

This gives you enough room to earn a healthy return in terms of cash flow from your property. It also gives you enough wiggle room in case things go wrong. Keep in mind that NOI calculations don't include mortgage payment. That is not an expense since you're gaining ownership of the asset, progressively, as you make those payments.

Turnkey investors and house hackers usually try to bring the NOI as close to the mortgage payment as possible to reduce their debt burden.

Cash Flow

All real estate investors prioritize cash flow to a greater extent than capital gains, because cash flow makes it cheaper for them to own the property. As I described earlier, the cash flow you earn from rental income reduces your mortgage debt burden every month.

For this reason, you need to record and track your cash flow at all times. Using the 50% rule of thumb helps massively with this because cash outflows can be erratic. For example, you won't be spending the same amount of money every single month on maintenance. Neither is your property going to be vacant every month.

You still need to account for these expenses and build a buffer into your finances. Typically, landlords stash six months' worth of rental payments in the bank so as to overcome any emergencies.

Your net cash flow from the property, after you take mortgage payments into account, will most likely be slightly negative. This isn't a bad thing. Remember you're paying that money to own an asset that will appreciate in value. Your objective should be to reduce the net cash outflow as much as possible.

Return on Investment

Also called ROI or cash on cash return, this is an important figure for investors to consider. This calculation differs depending on the type of investment strategy you employ. In the case of turnkey rental investing, you want to focus on the amount of cash you've placed in the property.

If you've financed it, then your investment in the property amounts to the down payment, closing costs, and the amount you spent on making any repairs to it before renting it out. Maintenance repairs are operating expenses and should not be included in the investment amount.

The way to calculate your cash on cash return is to divide your NOI by the investment amount. This gives you your ROI. The same method is used to calculate ROI in case of house hacking as well.

There are investment options that allow you to invest in real estate via the stock market. In this case, your ROI is calculated in two parts. The first part is the capital gains you earn from the appreciation of the stock price. The second is the yield.

Capital gains is easy enough to calculate. Simply subtract the purchase price from the current price and multiple this by the number of shares you've bought. Divide this number by the amount of money you invested in the stock. This is your capital gain appreciation.

Yield is calculated by adding the total cash distributions you receive from the stock (called dividends), and dividing the sum by the amount you invested in the stock. Over the long run, capital gains will be larger than the yield. However, the yield provides you with good income, much like how you earn rental income from a property.

Capitalization Rate

Also called the cap rate, this is a number that a lot of investors pay attention to. Every neighborhood has an average cap rate that investors try to achieve. The cap rate is the NOI divided by the price of the property. If the property is worth $100,000 and if the NOI is $6000, the cap rate is six percent. Given that property prices appreciate every year, landlords seek to raise the NOI as well. They do this by raising rents every year. Thus, the cap rate remains the same even if the NOI and property values fluctuate.

Total ROI

This number isn't referred to very much but it's usually calculated when you realized your capital gains from the property. In other words, it's relevant only when you sell the property and acts as a scorecard of sorts. On a day-to-day basis, paying attention to your ROI/cash on cash return, is far more important. The calculation of total ROI is straightforward. Subtract your investment from the total gains you've earned from the property over the years, and divide this by the cost.

Chapter 3:

Real Estate Investment

Trusts

Now that you have a good handle on the basics of real estate investment, it's time to dive right into the first method of online real estate investment. These are real estate investment trusts or REITs. REITs are one of the oldest, alternative, real estate investment methods and have been around since the 1960s.

They rose in popularity in the 1970s when the United States suffered from an energy crisis. The prices of oil rose astronomically and as a result, interest rates had to be hiked to a scarcely believable 11%. This meant a regular deposit in the bank was generating more money than the stock market was.

Investors sought alternative means of investment, away from the stock market. Ironically, they found it right within the market itself, but in a different asset class. While the stocks of most companies are exposed to sectors such as technology, infrastructure, utilities and so on, REITs are exposed to the real estate market.

They're different from the stocks of companies such as those that build homes, or big-box retailers like Home Depot. Those companies depend on real estate demand as well, but the impact of property prices on their stock is secondary. Here's what I mean.

If the prices of real estate fall and demand increases, Home Depot is going to witness an increase in demand for the items they sell. This means more profits for them. However, Home Depot has its own costs to consider. If it happens to be a poorly run company, its competitor, Lowe's, can make more money from the increased demand. This means Lowe's stock will rise higher over the long term.

The company's own financial situation comes in between the investor and real estate demand. A REIT removes this barrier by directly transferring all rental income yields to you, as much as possible. Here's how they work.

Lowe's and Home Depot have to pay taxes to the government on all of their profits. REITs don't have to. Their corporate structure ensures that they pay zero corporate taxes. This results in a windfall for them. However, there's a catch. In order to pay zero taxes, they need to distribute 90% of their profits back to investors.

Therefore, those who buy shares of REITs, receive 90% of the company's profits as dividends throughout the year. This means the dividends are substantial and are greater in amount than normal dividend paying stocks.

So what do REITs do and why do they even exist? The answer lies in the way property is developed. The average property developer or home building company requires a ton of cash to finance their projects. Their aim is to borrow money, build a project, and then sell those properties to people in order to service their debt, while also making a profit.

Home building companies thus experience a lot of volatility. If they borrow too much, they can make more money, but they're also exposed to a lot of risk in case demand for homes falls. If they borrow too little, they'll be placing too much of their own money in the project, and even if it comes off, they'll make too little in terms of ROI.

To a property developer, cash is everything. Once they've built the property, their aim is to sell all of the units as fast as possible. This isn't possible, though.

People buy properties at different times and, as a result, the developer witnesses intermittent cash flow. So how do they solve this problem? How can they offload all the units and recover their cash?

This is where a REIT comes in. REITs purchase the entire property from the developer and in turn, seek to make a profit by either reselling those units for a higher price, or by collecting rent from those properties. Most REITs seek to earn rent from the properties they own.

In some cases, REITs are affiliated or are group companies of large developers. This way the developer holds on to their property, and through accounting trickery, they manage to raise even more funds for their next development. However, this is irrelevant for us.

A REIT is a really, large landlord. They maintain the property and collect rent from it. They can invest in as many properties as they like, and in some cases will even invest in off-plan properties. These are properties that are still under construction. Such properties are considered risky since the developer might run out of cash.

However, the increased risk is accompanied by a huge rise in capital gains once the property is finished. The REIT sells shares of itself in the stock market and this is where you can buy them. Since the REIT is obligated to pay 90% of its profits to you, you're effectively earning the rental income from all of the properties the REIT owns.

Keep in mind that, despite being a more direct investment in rental income from properties, REITs don't transfer 90% of rental income to you directly. Given that they're companies too, they have costs. Therefore, you're receiving 90% of the rental income minus REIT costs.

You also own shares of the company, and do not have a claim over the underlying properties. Those are owned by the REIT itself. Therefore, you aren't a landlord in the traditional sense. You're still a stock market investor, albeit one with a huge and almost direct exposure to real estate.

Advantages

While not owning physical property might seem like a huge disadvantage, there are many advantages to investing in REITs. You'll find that these will override any other shortcomings of this form of investment.

Cost of Entry

Physical real estate investment requires you to invest at least five figures upfront, in the form of down payment and closing costs. This is a prohibitive sum for most people and it isn't as if you can draw upon this amount of money without planning for it many years beforehand.

With REITs this isn't the case. Since they're publicly traded like stocks, the average REIT costs somewhere between $20 to $150. Of course, there are REITs that cost a lot more and some that cost less, just as there are stocks that cost either pennies or hundreds of thousands.

It depends on how profitable the REIT is. Don't make the mistake of thinking that an expensive REIT is somehow better than a cheap one. It is in the REITs interest to keep its stock fully liquid.

Liquid here refers to the ease with which the stock can be traded. If the price of the stock is high, fewer people will be willing to trade it. Therefore, most companies perform what is called a split of their stock. They divide a single share with $100 (for example) into two shares worth $50. If you owned one share, you now own two.

This keeps the market value of the company the same but reduces the share price. This builds liquidity and keeps everyone happy. Thanks to this, the barrier of investment in REITs is low.

Liquidity

Speaking of which, liquidity is one of the biggest advantages of investing in REITs. Let's say you own a physical property and want to cash it in. You'll have to place it up for sale on the market and will need to field multiple offers. You'll need to negotiate prices and wait for the buyer to get approved for a mortgage.

The buyer might get back to you and ask for repairs or enhancements. Alternatively, they might request that you pay a portion of closing costs in lieu of repairs. You'll then need to wait for the money from escrow to arrive into your bank account. The entire process is heavy with paperwork, and it takes anywhere from a month to a year to offload physical property.

In the meantime, if you owned a REIT and needed to sell your holdings to make some cash, all you would have done is clicked a button. The liquidity inherent in REITs makes them really easy to buy and sell. I've highlighted the selling process above but the same point applies to the buying process as well.

If you have cash lying sound that you want to invest in real estate then you can simply buy more REITs by clicking a button. No lengthy mortgage approvals or anything of the kind!

Cash Flow

One of the biggest selling points of REITs is that they provide high levels of cash flow. This is in comparison to dividend-paying stocks. Historically, stocks have yielded around one to two percent. REITs have yielded around three to four percent (Historical REIT Spreads: Dividend Yields vs. U.S. Treasuries, 2019).

In addition to this, the real estate market moves in a different cycle from the stock market. An investor who has equal exposure to both stocks and REITs thus has a portfolio that can withstand downturns a lot better. This makes REITs an attractive source of both capital gains and cash flow.

Combine the higher-than-average cash flow with the ease of entering the investment, and you can see why so many investors prefer REITs over physical real estate.

Diversified

Let's say you buy a physical property. You own the place for sure but are now exposed to the rhythms of the local real estate market. Even if the entire country's real estate market does well, it isn't guaranteed that your property will witness a price rise. Local factors play an outsized role in determining returns, as I've mentioned earlier.

Your money is highly concentrated on one property. You live and die with it, so to speak. It would be great if you could somehow reduce the risk of this concentration. This is where REITs help. REITs usually hold multiple properties across various locations.

These properties have been carefully chosen and vetted prior to investment. So, with a single purchase of a REIT's share, you're buying exposure to all of these properties. Much like how a real estate component of your portfolio hedges your stock portion, the mixture of properties in a REIT helps you diversify your holdings.

You're not dependent on a single source of investment anymore. Diversification does reduce your potential for outsized returns. However, it also eliminates any chances of making outsized losses. Your capital is thus preserved a lot better than it is with physical real estate ownership.

Professional Management

I mentioned that REIT properties are carefully chosen and vetted. This is an important feature to note. Imagine if you had your very own team of property experts, looking out for the best opportunities to invest in. In return all it would cost you to employ them is a one-time fee of $50.

This is what you're getting with a REIT investment. You're getting access to professional management who have been around for a long time and know what they're doing. All you have to do is put your money in the REIT and collect your dividend checks. You can even choose to reinvest your dividends automatically, at no additional cost, to further boost your investment returns.

These are the primary advantages of REITs as an investment. There are a few disadvantages as well, and I've mentioned some of them before. Let's look at them in more detail.

Disadvantages

As great as REITs are, there is a tradeoff between the advantages and the disadvantages. After all, there isn't a single investment opportunity on the planet that gives you 100% risk-free money. Take a look at these disadvantages and check to see if you're willing to put up with them in return for the points discussed earlier.

Low Levels of Growth

Something that hobbles most REITs is that the level of capital gains they experience can be a lot lower than the average stock. While historically, REITs have appreciated at a rate greater than stocks, this isn't true for every single REIT out there. Given that they're paying out 90% of their profits, there isn't much room left for reinvestment.

This means the REIT's capital gains are tied to the gains witnessed in the properties they own. If REITs could reinvest, even a fraction of the 90% gains they payout, they could reinvest it into more properties and boost capital gains massively. The slightly reduced dividend yield would be justified in such cases.

However, the law prohibits them from doing so. If you're looking for capital gains appreciation on a large scale, then REITs are not the instruments of choice. While they will increase, on average, thanks to the property market's appreciation, the average common stock holds more capital gains potential than the average REIT.

This also means that the REIT's management needs to be on top of their expenses and cash outflows. If the number of dividends they're paying decreases, the stock price usually tumbles a long way down. This means that the task of managing a REIT is a delicate one that needs a sure hand.

Taxes

Perhaps the most confusing portion of REIT investment is taxes. I'm not talking about taxes for the company. Your own tax return is going to be a little complicated. This isn't a disadvantage as much as it is a matter of education. REIT dividends are composed of two types of payments: Ordinary dividends and Return of Capital or ROC.

Ordinary dividends are taxed at the same rate as your marginal tax bracket. ROC is a bit more complex. These are treated as capital gains, and as a result, they're deferred. When you sell the REIT, you will pay taxes on the difference between this adjusted cost basis and the selling price.

Here's a simple example to illustrate how this works. Let's say you purchase a REIT for $100. After a year it pays you an ordinary dividend of $2 and ROC of $1. You will pay income tax on the $2 distribution. The ROC reduces your cost basis by $1 to $99. As far as the IRS is concerned, you've bought this REIT for $99.

Let's say the price is now $110 and you wish to sell it after receiving these dividends. If this was a regular stock, your profit would be calculated as being (110-

100) $10. However, thanks to the ROC reducing your cost basis, your capital gains are now (110-99) $11. You will pay capital gains taxes on this amount.

The great thing about ROC is that if you never sell a REIT, you won't pay taxes on it ever. It'll keep reducing your cost basis until your effective price is zero. After that, you'll pay capital gains taxes on the ROC. However, if you pass the REIT investment onto your heirs after your death, their cost basis readjusts to the price the REIT was on the day of your passing.

Thus, they get to earn the ROC component until they decide to sell it. It's a bit complicated but when done right, REITs hold a few tax advantages for the investor.

Operational Control

REITs are companies and you're a shareholder. This means you don't have any operational control over the company. You can express your wishes through a vote but this is just one among a million. While you can earn dividends passively through REITs, you cannot count on management listening to you. That's the trade off you have with REITs.

This means you're entirely dependent on management. As I mentioned earlier, this is a tough task and you need to evaluate them thoroughly before investing money in the REIT. This disadvantage isn't present with physical real estate. For better or worse, you're in charge fully.

If you want, you can carry out certain tasks that boost the value of your property and bring in more rent. You can't do this with a REIT. You're entirely dependent on management understanding what's going on.

This might be tough for some investors to swallow. If you have a large amount of money to invest and don't mind a more active form of investment, physical real estate might be a better choice for you.

Fees

Unlike common stocks, REITs charge fees. Management has to pay 90% of profits out, and this means there isn't a lot of money left to pay themselves. Thus, almost every REIT out there charges management fees. It isn't just management fees, but rather a variety of fees that the investor ends up paying.

You can think of these fees as being the cost of your investment. Management fees usually contain two components: A base fee that is between 0.25% to one percent of the principal invested, and a performance fee that can be as much as 20% of the profits earned during the year.

If the REIT acquires new property, it will charge investors an acquisition fee of one percent of capital. If it sells a property, there is a divestment fee of 0.5%. As you can see, compared to common stock investment and even physical real estate, there are many fees to pay.

However, even if all of these fees are added up, they still come to less than the closing costs on physical real estate. Closing costs range from three to five percent of the property's value. Since your down payment is your cash investment in the property, closing costs can amount to as much as 30-50% of your principal in fees.

Granted, closing costs are one-time only, while REIT fees are recurring. However, over the course of time, you'll find that these fees even out. Combine this fact with the low barrier to entry, REITs offer advantages over physical real estate investment.

Market Risks

Despite being linked to real estate, REITs still represent stock ownership in a company. This makes them vulnerable to broad stock market risks. If the market goes through some crisis, then REITs could be affected as well. Usually, the prices of REITs will correct themselves over time, but in the short term, they do fluctuate according to the whims of the stock market.

Types of REITs

There are different types of REITs you can invest in. Given that these are professionally managed, you can think of a REIT as being a real estate property fund. Management decides what kind of properties and area they should be targeting and you can choose to invest in them if you like the sound of it.

As I mentioned earlier, REITs have steadily yielded around three to four percent historically. Their rate of return (capital gains) over the past 100 years has been close to 12.5%. This is in comparison to the broad stock market average gain of around seven to eight percent.

Clearly, REITs have outperformed stocks. However, there's a caveat to this performance. Real estate values in America rose considerably over that period and the bubble burst in 2007. Since then, the stock market has matched REITs and has outperformed it comfortably in some instances.

REIT yields are usually compared to Treasury yields to determine the state of the REIT market. Treasuries refer to the bonds that are issued by the U.S. Government. These are the most stable forms of debt in the world. When you buy a bond you earn a steady interest rate and your principal is returned to you at the end of the bond's term.

REITs function like bonds in many ways. The dividend is like an interest payment, and when you sell the REIT, you earn your principal back with capital gains as well, potentially. The difference between the yields of these two instruments is called the yield spread.

Historically, this has hovered around 1.5%. REITs have yielded this much more than Treasuries over the past 100 years (Case, 2017). Yields higher than this number indicate an undervalued REIT market. After all, yields rise when prices fall. If the spread widens, it means REIT yields have risen faster than treasury yields have. This means REIT prices have reduced faster.

Similarly, if the yield spread is lower, it means REITs are overvalued. The relationship isn't one-to-one like this. There might be conditions that are causing such over and under valuation. However, it forms a starting point for you to begin looking into individual REITs to invest in.

If analyzing every single REIT out there sounds tedious to you, you can opt to invest in an index fund that tracks REITs. An index fund tracks a basket of REIT stocks and therefore gives you exposure to the entire REIT industry instantly. You can invest in REIT index funds that track residential stocks, in ones that track commercial real estate, and so on.

This is a great way to automate your REIT investing. You'll still earn the dividends paid out by REITs through the index fund. The downside is you'll earn average to slightly above average returns. This is because your portfolio will be restricted to a wide variety of REITs and the outperformance of a single REIT won't have much of an impact on your overall investment.

The upshot is that you'll insulate yourself from significant underperformance. As with everything, the more risk you're willing to absorb, the greater your rewards will be.

Broadly speaking, there are three kinds of REITs you can invest in. While REITs can be classified on the basis of the kinds of properties they invest in, a better way to classify them is on the basis of their business model. The three types of REITs are:

1. Equity REITs
2. Mortgage REITs
3. Hybrid REITs

Equity REITs

The business model of these REITs is to act as a landlord and collect rent from their tenants. These REITs are solely focused on purchasing properties that provide high levels of cash flow. They carry out maintenance and other related tasks and pass 90% of their profits onto you.

Equity REITs can choose to invest in different kinds of properties. Some REITs invest solely in residential buildings. Others invest only in single-family homes. Still some more invest only in commercial property and shopping malls. There is a wide variety of investment objectives when it comes to the type of property being bought.

Equity REITs offer investors the chance to concentrate their holdings across both property classes and location. For example, you can invest in a REIT that purchases senior-living or assisted-living facilities in the Northeast United States. You can invest in a REIT that purchases land and leases it back to marijuana companies.

You can invest in REITs that buy land to lease it to communications companies to build cell phone towers on. There is no limit to the kind of property a REIT purchases and on how it chooses to monetize it. Make sure you do your research according to the points listed in the next section where I'll discuss analyzing REITs.

Mortgage REITs

Mortgage REITs or mREITs are a slightly riskier proposition. Their business model makes a lot of sense and it is something that many physical real estate investors gravitate towards at some point. Owning a property can be a headache sometimes. Your tenants won't pay on time and you'll need to constantly make sure it is well taken care of.

What if you could simply be the bank instead? You sit back and collect rent on the property while the tenant or builder takes care of the maintenance. You loan your money out as a bond and simply collect interest payments. In case you're financing a rehabber or a flipper, you could even opt to take a cut of the profits when the property is sold.

This sounds great as a business model, but it requires expertise to pull off. Specifically, you need to evaluate risk very well. Is a person creditworthy enough? Can they make payments on time? And so on.

Now multiply this difficulty by 100 and you have an mREIT. These companies use different methods of financial engineering and in the past have used derivatives to boost returns. The use of derivatives led to mREITs being hit massively in the financial crisis in 2008 and a large number of them went belly up.

Having said that, their business model does result in a great amount of profits since their overheads are low.

All they do is lend money. There's no maintenance tasks or anything else that they do. They collect their interest payments and pass 90% of their profits onto you.

This form of investment is better suited to more experienced investors. If you wish to capture the gains of this business model, wait until you're making a good amount of money from your other passive, real estate investments before jumping into these instruments.

Hybrid REITs

As the name suggests, these REITs combine the business models of both equity and mortgage REITs. These have grown in number over the previous decade, partly because high levels of leverage among mREITs caused Armageddon in the REIT market. This led to mREITs rethinking their leverage, and they diversified into equity models.

It's best for the investor to stick to equity REITs. Hybrids don't offer any major advantage and only offer the risks of both business models. The losses from the mREIT side of things can overwhelm the equity side thanks to the leverage being used to lend money.

Private Versus Public

There is another distinction that you should be aware of when it comes to REITs. There are public as well as private REITs. Within the realm of public REITs, there are two categories. These are publicly traded REITs and publicly non-traded REITs. As their names suggest one type is traded regularly and the other isn't.

Technically speaking, non-traded REITs are still available for purchase. It's just that they're not as liquid as fully traded REITs. Private REITs are offered to institutional and registered investors only. A registered investor is one that is worth at least a million dollars after their primary residence's value is removed from the equation.

The average investor doesn't have to worry about these types of distinctions. Simply stick to liquid REITs and you'll do just fine.

Analyzing REITs

Analyzing the financial worthiness of a REIT for investment is a simpler task than analyzing a company. This is because REITs have a very well-defined business model, and aren't subject to a business sector's economics as companies often are. This means all you need to do is focus on a few individual metrics and you'll do well.

Before we get into the individual terms to look at, you need to understand a little thing called GAAP. GAAP stands for Generally Accepted Accounting Principles and is the framework upon which all accounting exists. It is a set of rules that governs how companies must account for their income, assets and cash flow.

GAAP is meant to serve a wide variety of industries and, as a result, it has a few quirks that make REIT accounting nonsensical at times. Perhaps nonsensical is too strong a word, but it certainly does result in numbers that make no sense. The biggest anomaly that GAAP causes on REIT company books is caused by a thing called depreciation.

Depreciation refers to the rate at which companies write down their assets. Let's say you bought a TV yesterday for $500. It's a great TV and you love it. You continue using it for five years. In the fifth year someone asks you how much you want for it. How do you determine what's a fair price?

The easiest way is to look at the prices five-year-old TVs are commanding in the market and price your TV around the same. You'll also notice that your TV is not worth anywhere near $500 now since five years have passed. This is because everything loses value over time thanks to wear and tear.

What if you decide to not sell the TV? If someone were compiling a list of your assets, what would they then value the TV at? Constantly checking the market for the prices of used TVs is tedious and what's more, it still is an estimate. You won't know what it's true worth is until you sell it.

To make this easy for companies to do, accounting introduced the concept of depreciation. The TV you bought is written down over the years until its value is zero. It could be reduced by 10% every year until it is ascribed zero value by year 11. This reduction in value is considered an expense by accountants.

However, it isn't a cash expense. If your TV reduces in value from year one to year two, it isn't as if you're paying cash out of your pocket to someone. It exists solely on paper. For many industries this makes sense, and it makes their books easier to analyze. However, it makes zero sense for REITs.

Consider a REIT's primary asset: property. What happens to property that is well-maintained over a long enough timespan? It appreciates in value! Yet, GAAP tells us to depreciate it. As a result, REIT companies incur huge depreciation expenses on their books.

This expense is subtracted from their income and as a result, net income levels are low. They're so low in fact, that the dividend paid routinely exceeds it. Some investors get alarmed by this and think that the REIT is losing money. However, it's just an illusion caused by GAAP.

Cash Flow

The correct way to begin analyzing a REIT is to look at its cash flow. Much like how rental investors pay attention to the NOI and cap rates, you need to look at these equivalent numbers for the REIT.

The cash flow statement holds all the information you're looking for. Pay attention to the income from operations number. Subtract the capital expenditures (which is another line item) from it, to arrive at the free cash available. Make sure the dividend payment is around 90% of this number.

A percentage that is higher than 90% indicates that the REIT is overextending itself. Free cash flow is the first line item you'll need to calculate. More specifically, you want to look at the trend of free cash flow over the years. An erratic cash flow with regularly overextended dividend payments is a bad sign.

Funds From Operations

Also called FFO, this is a calculation that many REIT investors take into account. Once you've calculated free cash flow, you need to look down to the last section titled 'cash flow from investing activities.' It might not be named like this exactly. The point is this section contains the cash the company earned from the sale of properties.

Compare the free cash flow to this number. Ideally, you want the latter to be a lot smaller than the former.

Usually, companies that sell properties to bring cash in, tend to have overextended dividend payments. Remember that in order to qualify as a suitable long-term investment, you want your REIT company to be paying close to 90% or slightly more than 90% of its free cash flow.

An alternative calculator of FFO is to subtract non-cash expenses from net income, and then further subtract gains from selling assets. The net income is listed on the income statement. Instead of doing this, simply look at the cash flow statement which does this for you automatically.

Another number that is related to the FFO is the Adjusted Funds From Operations or AFFO (Kenton, 2019). You'll notice from the calculation I mentioned (the net income one) that FFO doesn't contain the capital expenditures element. AFFO is calculated by subtracting the capital expenditures from the FFO.

Generally speaking, REIT investors divide these two numbers out separately. However, from a business perspective, it makes no sense to do this. Ultimately, your aim is to figure out how profitable a REIT is. This can only be done by subtracting costs from revenues and comparing that to distributions.

Thus, don't waste your time on the income statement and head straight to the cash flow section. This is what every physical, real estate investor focuses on and you should as well.

Net Asset Value

REITs are well known for their high dividend payments, and as a result, their share prices can be inflated. The key for you as an investor is to stay away from overinflated REITs. This will result in potentially lower capital gains and a lower yield. After all, an inflated asset can only go so high.

True bargains in REITs are hard to come by. However, you can purchase them when they're close to their net asset value or NAV. This is calculated by subtracting the value of all liabilities from the asset values.

Both of these numbers are provided in the balance sheet in their respective sections. Subtract total liabilities from total assets and you have this number. Divide it by the total number of shares outstanding (also on the balance sheet) and you'll have the NAV per share.

Compare this to its price and look at the premium. Is it too high compared to the other REITs? All financial analysis software usually lists comparable companies and competitors. Look at their share price to NAV, and figure out whether this premium is justified.

A REIT that is selling at a significant premium when compared to its competitors is either over hyped or it's a truly well run company. Investment success depends on how good of a price you can capture upon entry.

The closer it is to the true NAV, the better. Of course, you will find some REITs selling at below NAV.

In these cases, you should investigate why this is the case. The market doesn't allow such inefficiencies to remain for long, so you need to investigate why this is the case. Perhaps its property values have dipped massively or perhaps it has suffered some external shock.

Don't use a NAV discount to price as an automatic entry method.

Concentration

Which types of real estate has the REIT invested in? What are the prospects of that sector? For example, the REIT might have invested in office buildings but if the entire world is now moving towards remote work, how lucrative can this possibly be?

You don't have to be an investment genius to figure out the prospects of a real estate sector. Simply read the news and stay up to date with all information that is out there. If a REIT is diversified across the country then you have less homework to do. If it's focusing solely in a particular area, then you will need to become familiar with the dynamics of that particular area.

REITs and other publicly traded companies, file a document called the 10-K with the Securities and

Exchange Commission (SEC), which lists their financial performance and the state of their business. This information is available for free online at the SEC's EDGAR database.

The 10-K contains a section called 'Risks' in the beginning, and this is where the company's management lists all of the risks that affect the business. Take your time reading this section. Look at all the risks involved and determine whether you're willing to stomach them.

Management

As I mentioned earlier, so much of the success of your investment depends on the quality of management. Take a look at what their qualifications are and how long they've been in the business. How well have they grown operations since inception, and do they discuss risks to their business openly?

The 10-K contains a section titled Management's Discussion and Analysis. Read this to see how open and transparent management is when it comes to discussing the issues around their business. A management that honestly admits its shortcomings is much better than one that thumps its chest at every possible opportunity.

This is subjective, of course. Everyone has different levels of risk they can stomach. Find the ones that suit you and act accordingly. Whatever you do, don't go chasing high dividend yields in REITs. Some investors begin with this as a starting point and don't look at anything else.

They search for REITs yielding eight percent or more and fail to remember that high yields can be caused by low share prices. If a REIT is facing a tough time, and if its share prices have fallen, yields will go higher even if the dividend payments remain the same.

It will take a little time but the time investment is worth it. Stick to reading the 10-K and invest accordingly.

で

Chapter 4

Real Estate ETFs and

Mutual Funds

REITs are the primary source of nontraditional investment in real estate. However, there are two other options that the stock market provides. These are real estate exchange-traded funds (ETFs) and mutual funds.

A mutual fund is something you've probably heard of already.

These are actively managed funds that concentrate on particular sectors or asset classes. In the case of real estate, mutual funds can invest in either properties themselves, or in companies that are active in this field, such as REITs. Usually, a mutual fund invests in other companies and doesn't take direct ownership of the property.

Mutual funds also have the concept of NAV attached to them. Their assets are priced once every day and investors purchase it at that price before the market closes. Their prices don't fluctuate freely in the market like REIT prices do. This usually doesn't pose any significant risk to long-term investors.

You'll find that mutual funds always have lots of liquidity and you won't have any issues entering or exiting your investment. They happen to be one of the oldest types of managed investment funds in the world, and as such are very safe investment vehicles, outside of market risk factors.

The other type of investment vehicle I'll be talking about is an ETF. An ETF is similar to a mutual fund except for the fact that it trades freely on the market like a REIT does. This means you'll have to constantly keep track of the premium-to-discount value of the price to NAV.

In case the markets become volatile, ETF prices will jump to unreasonable levels. This is a simple, particular risk of investing in them. However, it's confined only to market entry and isn't applicable to any other point of time in your investment. Like mutual funds, ETFs have high levels of liquidity and can be bought and sold freely.

ETFs can have a large number of strategies that underlie them. They're essentially hedge funds for ordinary people. Most ETFs adopt a passive investment strategy where they follow an underlying index, like the ones I spoke about in the previous chapter. These ETFs make for excellent passive investments, if you don't wish to engage in individual REIT analysis.

Both mutual funds and ETFs pool money to invest in certain strategies. Despite this underlying similarity, there are some differences between them that you should be aware of.

Differences

The decision of whether to invest in an ETF or a mutual fund involves running through the differences between the two forms of investment and seeing which one suits you better. In no particular order, here are the differences between them.

Tradability

Mutual funds are priced once a day and, as an investor, the price that is listed is what you'll pay no matter what happens in the market. At the end of the day, the fund's NAV is repriced and that is the price available the following day. ETFs trade freely and their prices fluctuate.

This single-price versus liquid-price feature brings its own advantages and disadvantages. Let's begin with the advantages. When price is stationary, you're less likely to want to trade in and out of it constantly. As I mentioned earlier, one of the keys to successful real estate investment is the ability to hold on for long periods of time.

The markets are volatile and news often affects short-term price movements. The financial media does the average investor no favors. In the name of breaking news, they simply give you reasons to trade emotionally. In fact, most investors are best off if they simply switch off the news channels and focus on a few simple things.

Given that a mutual fund isn't going to move during the day, this frees up the investors time to do other things, and most importantly, it gives them the opportunity to get out of their own way. A good example of this is investor behavior during so-called flash crashes.

A flash crash is a market crash that occurs over the course of a few minutes. The increasing amount of algorithmic participation in the market has ensured that flash crashes occur with increasing frequency. Once such crashes occur, the news media grabs onto it as if the world is ending.

During such crashes, the price of pretty much every tradable asset in the market drops massively over the course of a minute or so. This includes ETFs. Investors who know they can trade in and out of their holdings, will be tempted to remove money from their investments because of sheer panic.

You could be the most rational person in the world but when panic strikes, most people fold. By removing the possibility of trading at different prices during the day, you're less likely to sabotage yourself. Panic usually causes people to sell low or to get out of their investments when they should be thinking of getting in.

Mutual funds remove this danger through their single price NAV model. It also removes the possibility of the price moving too far away from its NAV. ETFs almost never trade at their NAV, due to the constant fluctuation of prices. Furthermore, many people actively speculate in them due to price fluctuations.

This means a long-term investor needs to be very careful of what price they're paying on entry. You could be paying too much due to short-term sentiment. This reduces the odds of you making a large return over the long term. However, the flip side of this is you can exit during moments of short-term irrationality for a high price.

This isn't possible with a mutual fund. If you feel that you would like the relative pricing freedom that ETFs offer, then you're best off staying away from mutual funds. Mutual funds are best suited for people who want to simplify their investing to bare-bones levels and want zero distractions from their goal.

I'm not trying to say that you cannot invest successfully using ETFs. It's just that if you're prone to making emotionally rash decisions, then mutual funds might be the better bet for you.

Fees

Fees are a major point of difference between most mutual funds and ETFs. Remember how I said that a lot of ETFs are passively managed? This means the fund's managers are simply following an index and are adjusting their portfolios accordingly. For example, let's say that an ETF is following an underlying index that tracks the five biggest REITs in the market.

All the ETF manager has to do is buy those five ETFs in equal amounts and make sure those distributions remain the same as they are in the index. Due to this, a lot of these ETFs are managed via an algorithm and not a human being. This helps keep costs low. After all, a machine doesn't demand a salary.

Typically, passive ETFs charge fees of 0.3 to 0.5% of the investment principal. That is an extremely low amount of fees and is far less than what a lot of mutual funds typically charge. The average mutual fund charges three to five percent of investment capital as fees.

This is because the mutual fund isn't merely seeking to replicate the performance of an index. Instead, it's objective is to outperform the market or sector specific index. However, the fund's manager gets paid whether they lose or make money. This hurts investment performance massively.

You can imagine how bad it would be if your investment made no money during an entire year and yet the manager charges you five percent of your investment principal as fees. Fees for what exactly? This is what caused the creation of another type of mutual fund called an index fund, along with ETFs.

Index funds, as their name suggests, aren't preoccupied with outperforming anything. They simply seek to match an index and work just like mutual funds in that their NAV is priced once a day. They don't trade at premiums or discounts as a result. Their expense ratios are lower than most ETFs as well.

The most popular index funds are offered by Vanguard which is a pioneer of the index investing methodology. Vanguard's funds (both ETFs and index funds) usually charge less than o.5% as expense fees. This makes them excellent picks for a passive investing strategy.

A lot of mutual funds also charge their investors what are called loading fees. This refers to a percentage of your principal that is charged right when you invest in the fund. Typically, this is around one percent of your invested amount. Thus, you're in the red right when you begin. Index funds don't charge any loading fees and there are other mutual funds that offer zero load plans.

Some funds even charge their investors a redemption fee. Mutual funds that run sophisticated strategies might impose what are called lockups on their investors. This means the investor cannot withdraw their money before a certain period unless they wish to pay additional fees as a penalty.

Overall, the fee profile of a mutual fund varies greatly from one manager to the next. You should take the time to study it if you're choosing to invest in them. In contrast, index funds and ETFs offer simple fee structures that can be readily understood by the common investor.

Investment Minimums

Mutual funds usually require a certain amount of minimum investment initially. For example, all of Vanguard's index funds usually require a $3,000 minimum investment. ETFs on the other hand do not have any investment minimums attached to them. You can purchase as little as one share.

This functions as the de facto minimum investment in an ETF, but with most ETFs priced between $30 to $200, this is far less than the amount needed for a mutual fund. Keep in mind that companies such as Vanguard offer both mutual fund and ETF versions of the same strategy for you to invest in.

Taxes

ETFs are pretty straightforward in terms of how they're taxed. All dividends that are paid by the ETF are taxed as ordinary income, and you'll pay the same rate as your marginal income tax rate. With mutual funds, it isn't as straightforward.

Mutual fund distributions include both capital gains as well as ordinary income components. In some distributions, one component could be zero with the other making up its entirety. In some cases, it could be an even split. Based on the type of distribution, you will end up paying different tax rates on them (Boyte-White, 2020).

Capital gains taxes are determined by whether they're short-term or long-term. Any investment that has been sold after holding on to it for at least a year, qualifies for a long-term capital gains tax. This tax rate is between zero to 20% and the exact tax rate you pay depends on your marginal income tax bracket.

Short-term capital gains, that is, gains from investments held for less than a year, are taxed at the same rate as income tax. In other words, ordinary income distributions and short-term capital gains are taxed at the same rates.

This makes the amount of tax due on these instruments different. You won't have to do any additional work since your broker will provide you with a statement that reflects these distributions. It's just that your amount of returns will vary.

For example, an investor who has bought an ETF and another that has bought an index fund version of the same ETF face different tax burdens. A distribution from the ETF is taxed as ordinary income no matter what. However, the distribution from the mutual fund might come in the form of long-term capital gains, and this reduces the amount of tax they have to pay.

On the flip side, if the mutual fund pays a raft of short-term capital gains distributions to the investor, then this will result in the same tax bill as the investor in the ETF. You must take into account the performance fees, as well as the tax trade-offs, when deciding to invest.

Look at the prospectus of the fund to determine the distribution history and check to see how this might have affected your taxes.

Advantages of ETFs and Mutual Funds

Why are ETFs and mutual funds a better bet for the average investor over individual REITs? It comes back to risk versus reward. Individual REITs have the potential to earn higher-than-market-average returns, but the flip side is that they can reduce in value as well. Furthermore, they're individual companies and you will be exposed to the vagaries of the way they do business by investing in them.

Most investors don't have the time to sit down and effectively analyze a company's prospects. This leads them to perform half-hearted analysis on them, and they don't fully understand the risks they're undertaking. ETFs and mutual funds remove this risk completely.

This happens due to the magic of diversification.

Diversification

When building a portfolio, there are two lines of thought. The first prescribes concentrating your portfolio between a few investments, while the other says that you should spread your risk out as much as possible. For example, Warren Buffett does not diversify his investments. When he likes a company, he loads up on it as much as possible.

Portfolio concentration works wonders when you're right about your investments. By investing a large amount of your portfolio in an opportunity, you stand to make huge gains when it comes off. It's how all great investors have made money in the markets. However, it has also caused many investors to go broke.

If you're wrong about the market, and if it goes the other way, a huge part of your portfolio is at risk. This means you're exposed to market risk at far higher levels than normal. In short, you live and die by the sword. A single mistake can cause you to lose tons of money. On the flip side, a single good decision will make you tons of money.

Portfolios such as these tend to be quite volatile, and to address this volatility, diversification was introduced as a means of reducing it. The thesis behind diversification is quite simple. The more you're spread your risk, the less power a single risky event has to destabilize your portfolio.

By spreading your eggs across many baskets, you're less dependent on a single basket remaining strong. Even if one does break, you can rely on the others. Thus, your risk is distributed. The downside of diversification is that you won't achieve much higher than market average returns.

If the underperformance of a single investment doesn't have the power to affect your portfolio, it stands to reason that over performance won't either. In fact, if you diversify too much, you'll end up earning nothing. This is because the parts of your portfolio that move up will be negated by the parts that move down. If no single item in your portfolio can affect it, it's not going to rise or fall in value.

Investors who have time to devote to the market, and conduct thorough analysis of companies, should concentrate their investments. This allows them to realize the full fruits of their labor. If you don't have the time, then diversification is your best bet. You will need to diversify intelligently, of course, instead of simply buying everything in sight.

Intelligent diversification means you'll need to find that sweet spot between properly diversified and over diversified. You want to maximize your gains to the extent that you'll earn market average returns, but won't diversify to the extent that you won't earn anything.

This means you need to spend time constructing and maintaining a portfolio. Time is what you didn't have, which is why you're considering diversification. It makes no sense to determine your diversification proportions by yourself. Thus, the best solution is to pay someone to do it and this is where ETFs and mutual funds come in.

By paying an expense fee, you manage to free up your time to do something else and leave professionals to handle your money. What's more, with the single click of a button you diversify accurately and gain exposure to market-average upside, with little, long-term downside, to the market.

I must mention that diversification will not guard you from losses. If the entire market declines, your portfolio will as well. It's just that the overall market in America has risen over the long term, thanks to the economic strength of the systems in this country. We can expect the same strength to continue for a while and this is why investing for the long term is the most profitable move.

Liquidity

If you choose to invest in large proportions into a single company's stock, you're exposing yourself to the liquidity, or lack of it, in that stock. You'll need to be careful when buying or selling it, since volumes might disappear at any moment. If the company has a bad earnings announcement, then you could be hit with a raft of sell orders that causes prices to crash.

This environment makes it very difficult for an individual investor to get in and out of their investment. This isn't always the case with an ETF. ETFs trade like stocks as well, but they tend to be far more liquid. This is because they're much bigger in size, thanks to the assets they manage, than the average REIT.

Also, ETFs attract a large number of investors, and this ensures there's always market for them. Mutual funds, as you've already learned, do not trade freely. Instead, their price is fixed at the NAV for that day, and investors trade at that price no matter what. The fund ensures there's always a market and can step in to buy units back if need be.

This removes a large amount of liquidity risk that investors could potentially face.

Tax Benefits

This advantage doesn't have to do with tax benefits as much as the pass-through nature of both investment types. You don't have to give up any of the tax features that REITs provide you with just because you're not investing in them directly.

ETFs and mutual funds simply pass these along to you. Therefore, you get the best of all worlds. Not only do you have a professional team managing your money, you also gain all of the tax benefits associated with them.

While this isn't a tax benefit per se, REITs have always been looked at as a hedge against inflation. This ties back to what you learned earlier about properties rising in value at the rate of inflation at the very least. Since REITs are tied directly to real estate values, their fortunes are tied to the inflation rate as well.

By investing in ETFs and mutual funds tied to REITs, you ensure that your investment will rise at least at the inflation rate. Thus, your money's purchasing power remains the same at the very least over the long term.

The biggest advantage of ETFs and mutual funds is that you get to save your time. Instead of trying to figure out where to invest and what to invest in, you simply click a button and let someone else do the work. In exchange, you pay a low expense fee (in the case of index funds and ETFs), which is reasonable considering the time you're saving.

What to Look for in an ETF

There are few things to look for in a real estate ETF that will help you quickly get a handle on what the fund is all about and how reliable it is. Let's look at them one by one.

Provider

The ETF provider is the financial institution that is issuing the fund. Typically, you'll see the following names quite a lot:

- iShares
- Fidelity
- JP Morgan
- Vanguard
- SPDR
- Schwab/Charles Schwab
- Nuveen
- Franklin Templeton
- T. Rowe Price

The last two firms on this list don't have huge REIT presence, but are high-quality issuers nonetheless. All of these firms have their own rich history and offer different philosophies when it comes to investment. For example, T. Rowe Price is famous for offering funds that achieve high rates of growth (or at least target them.)

Vanguard was the pioneer of low-cost investing, and you can expect their fund to have the lowest costs and expenses. iShares, as a company, looks far beyond the U.S. when it comes to investment opportunities and this means you can potentially gain exposure to international real estate, as well, by purchasing their ETFs.

You won't go wrong with any of these issuers. Stick to the ones in this list and don't stray far from it. If you have doubts about any particular issuer, conduct your research on them online and compare them to the companies on this list.

Assets

All of the issuers on that list issue multiple ETFs. It can be tough to pick the ones that are best suited for you. If you're just starting out with investing in REITs or funds, then sticking to the ones with assets above $500 million, is a good bet. This means the fund is of an adequate size.

It also means the manager has a good reputation and has created good gains for their investors up until that point. This increases the safety of your investment. A large asset base also gives the fund an advantage in terms of seizing opportunities.

More often than not, high quality REITs like pointing to the presence of a large ETF as an investor in them, to indicate to investors that they are a strong company. As a result, large funds witness many offers being brought to them, that smaller ETFs tend to miss out on.

This doesn't mean a smaller ETF will not make as much money as a large one. However, you can count on the fund receiving some good deals. Large asset sizes and prestigious issuers also mean the fund can throw more resources at research and on unearthing more opportunities.

Stick to the biggest funds offered by the issuers above. You'll find that they're as big as a few billion in most cases.

Age

The older the fund is, the more market cycles it has witnessed, and the more experienced the manager is when it comes to dealing with new surprises. This one doesn't need too much explanation.

Look for funds that are at least five years old. This gives you enough of a track record to examine.

Liquidity

You want your ETF to be as liquid as possible, since you don't want to be stuck with it when you wish to get out quickly. Unfortunately, there is no number you can look at to directly measure liquidity. However, there is a close substitute for this: Trading volume.

Trading volume is the amount of shares or units of a fund that were traded during a particular market session. Higher volumes indicate that there are more traders present in the fund and that there's a larger market for it. This indicates that there is likely going to be a larger band of prices that will be available for you to trade in.

Another knock on effect that large volumes have, is the tightening of the price spread. Prices in the market aren't singular. Most investors think of them of being so, but in fact, all securities in the market trade at two prices. There is a price you pay to buy the security and a price you pay when selling.

The latter is called the bid and the former is called the ask. The difference between them is called the spread. The closer or tighter the spread is, the more liquid an instrument is, thanks to the presence of many traders who wish to transact in it. Illiquid instruments often have side spreads that make it difficult to trade in and out of them.

Large volumes result in a tightening of the spread and as a result, you'll be able to rest assured that there is enough demand for your ETF. Look for a minimum traded volume of 200,000 every day. Any number above this is adequate in terms of volume.

Expense Ratio

By default, you want to pick the lowest expense ratio, relative to performance. Choosing the lowest ratio is easy enough. Simply pick the lowest number. It's the second part that trips everyone up. How do you pick the lowest number relative to performance? The idea is to look at the performance of the fund relative to its expenses.

A fund that performs well, and tracks its underlying index well, might justify a higher expense ratio. A lower expense ratio might end up costing you more, if the

ETF doesn't manage to replicate the underlying index well.

The best place to begin is to look at the tracking difference between the fund and the underlying index. The tracking difference refers to the difference between the ETF's performance (NAV) and the underlying index's returns.

All funds list this on their information page. You'll want to pick the ones that have the smallest gap to the index. Note that most ETFs won't replicate performance exactly. This happens because of trading fees and other costs involved with making transactions. Choose the ones with the lowest difference and pick the lowest expense ratios from this list.

Underlying Securities

When reading the fund's prospectus, make sure you pay attention to the underlying securities the ETF holds. Certain fund managers don't follow the underlying index exactly. They expand the investment brief of the fund and as a result, you'll see the ETF hold many more securities than the index.

Another reason for checking the underlying securities is to determine your sector exposure. In the case of a REIT fund, your primary exposure is going to be to real estate. However, look at the division between REITs versus companies that are active in the real estate space such as big box retailers, home builders etc.

If the fund's composition isn't something that you have in mind, then choose another one that sticks closely to the index.

What to Look for in a Mutual Fund

The points that I made just now, about what to look for in an ETF, largely apply to mutual funds as well. You want to look at the issuer of the fund as well as the management team in charge. There are a few additional points you must look at when it comes to mutual funds.

Track Record

While looking at the tracking difference, in the case of an ETF, is enough, you need to focus on the track record when it comes to a mutual fund. This is because a mutual fund is explicitly designed for outperformance. If it manages to underperform a relevant index, then it isn't very good.

There are different performance horizons you must look at. The fund's prospectus will highlight performance over a year, five years and 10 years if applicable. Every fund will also have what is called a benchmark index. This index measures the performance of the sector the fund is tied to.

Sometimes, mutual fund managers change their benchmarks or choose benchmarks that are easier to beat. In some cases this is justified, so a change by itself isn't a bad sign. Make sure you read the reasoning behind choosing the benchmark. If the fund manager's explanation doesn't make sense then stay away from it.

You want to view the mutual fund's performance in relation to the broad market. If the real estate market (which is measured via the U.S. REIT index) has witnessed a huge surge in performance over a decade, has the mutual fund exceeded it? Matching the benchmark index is not good enough.

If you wanted benchmark returns, then you could invest in an ETF for lower cost. The mutual fund needs to outperform, by at least the amount of fees you're paying the manager. Don't be swayed by negative returns or positive returns over time periods. It is the relative performance you want to pay attention to.

Fees

With mutual funds this is a big one. ETFs have low expense ratios, and they're typically under 0.5% of your principal. Mutual funds have a variety of fees, as I highlighted earlier. Make a note of all the fees they charge. These days many funds function as no-load or zero-load funds.

However, they make up for this through nonsensical redemption fees and other charges. Take the time to fully read the prospectus so that you understand how they work.

Turnover Ratio

The turnover ratio measures how often the fund manager buys and sells the securities in the mutual fund's portfolio. The higher the turnover ratio is, the greater will be the short-term capital gains. This means more taxes for you to pay. So watch out for higher turnover levels in funds.

You should compare this to the level of outperformance the fund manages. If the fund comfortably outperforms its index, the increased taxes and fees might still put you at a higher level of return. Keep this in mind.

Portfolio and Strategy

Like with ETFs, you want to be fully familiar with the mutual fund's strategy and how it allocates money. The fund manager will describe this in great detail in the prospectus. Often, mutual fund managers will stick to companies of a certain size. If you see the term 'blend' in the prospectus, this means they move across asset classes.

This isn't a bad or a good thing, it's just a feature. Make sure you understand what is being said. Mutual fund managers will also highlight the relative risk level inherent in the fund. This will be presented as a bar of sorts with higher values on the bar representing higher risk levels.

These measures are not a great way of understanding risk. True risk is you not understanding even the simplest and safest of investment strategies. Make sure you understand the strategy well and even the most complex of strategies will be worthy of investment.

Chapter 5:

Real Estate Crowdfunding

Crowdfunding has become an increasingly viable way for people to raise money for a variety of causes. While the majority of crowdfunding campaigns are used by companies to raise awareness about their products, or by individuals to raise funds for causes, over the course of this decade crowdfunding has expanded into other areas.

Real estate is no exception. These days you can invest in crowdfunded, real estate operations. Truth be told, the crowdfunding label that is attached to these types of investments is marketing hype. They're essentially private REITs and function in the same manner.

It's just that your investment in such a REIT is being facilitated by a technology company instead of a stock exchange. Hence, the label crowdfunding is attached to it to make it seem unique or more complex. It's pretty much the same as a regular REIT investment.

The crowdfunding model itself has a lot in common with the way shares are sold in the open market. Lots of people contribute small amounts of money and the project is funded. In the case of real estate, the capital necessary to make the deal happen is raised from a large pool of small investors.

The way it works is a bit different from investing in a REIT on the stock market. In the case of a publicly traded REIT, you're investing in the entire portfolio. With crowdfunded real estate, the deal sponsor advertises a single deal and you place your money in it.

Companies such as Fundrise are considered deal syndicators. In the real estate world, a syndicator is an entity that invests money into a project and finances. They can either invest on an equity basis or on a debt basis. I'll shortly explain what these terms mean. The syndicator seeks a rate of return from their investment.

As and when the project pays off its investors, the syndicator returns payments to their investors. The rate of return the investor realizes depends on the financials of the project. The syndicator gets paid by keeping some of the overall profit for themselves.

There are different ways of investing in crowdfunded real estate. Let's take a look at these now.

Types of Investments

There are two kinds of investments you can make into crowdfunded real estate. The first is debt and the other is equity. Both of these methods offer different advantages and their return profiles are also different. Let's take a look at equity investments first.

Equity

Anytime you hear the word equity mentioned in relation to investment, it means you're buying a share of the profits from the property. In the stock market equities refer to the shares of companies that are bought and sold daily. When it comes to real estate, it refers to receiving a share of the profits from the deal.

Here's how it works. The syndicator buys a property that is up for sale with the intention of leasing it out to renters. They take care of the maintenance of the property and so on, and pass on a portion of the rent to you. By doing this, they're functioning much like an equity REIT does.

As an investor, you profit from the rental payments that are made. An investment in an equity crowdfunded REIT can run for a long time. Technically, it will run until the property is sold by the syndicator. Every deal has different terms and the syndicator will describe how long they intend to hang onto the property.

The returns on equity deals generally tend to be higher because you're absorbing higher levels of risk from the deal. If the deal goes south, you won't get paid and you'll lose the money you've invested in it. There are different equity strategies that a company can take.

A popular investment strategy is to invest in neighborhoods that are slated for redevelopment by the city council or local government. These properties usually provide investors with certain advantages such as tax benefits and subsidies. By redeveloping these properties, the syndicator realizes a huge amount of capital gains. If they hang onto the property, they continue to earn rent from it, boosting their returns further.

Another strategy is to buy homes in neighborhoods that are witnessing increasing levels of population. Every metropolitan area and its surroundings, goes through cycles of population coming and going. By investing in homes or other types of property in these areas, and leasing them out for rent, the syndicator can earn steady rental returns.

All of these returns are passed onto you (less the syndicate's fees). Generally, the dividend yield on these investments are thought to be around 3.5% (according to Fundrise) and returns can be anywhere from five to 15%.

Something to keep in mind is that the advertised rate of return and real rate are two very different things. You'll often read about crowdfunded real estate investments that promise 15% returns per year. These are astronomical sums and happen to be a marketing creation.

Here's how such deals work. The syndicator buys a property and rehabs it. They then lease it for rent and build enough equity in it to qualify for a cash-out refinance. This usually takes around eight to 10 years (or more), depending on the kind of deal and property involved.

During this time, the investors of the syndicate are paid their share of rental returns and these amount to two to three percent of their investments. At the end of the deal, when the property is sold for hopefully a large capital gain, the investors receive their share of these gains.

The syndicator projects the market value of the property many years down the road, and then works backwards to determine a yearly rate of return. This is how the 15% number is arrived at. You will not receive 15% yearly like clockwork, despite advertising implying this to be the case. You'll receive a lump sum of capital gains at the end of the deal's term, if the market holds up according to the syndicator's projections.

This doesn't mean equity crowdfunding is bad in any way. It's just that you shouldn't buy the hype of some of these offerings that promise you astronomical returns. They might deliver good performance, but any syndicator that relies on such hype to generate funds is suffering from a lack of credibility in the market.

Thanks to the explosion of real estate crowdfunding, a number of syndicators have taken to YouTube and social media to advertise their deals. A bunch of them are nothing more than internet salesmen, who fill their channels with motivational videos that show how they went from rags to riches.

Be wary of such opportunities. Choose the right platforms to invest in and stay away from the loudmouths. I'll run through a list of the best platforms in the next chapter.

Debt

Debt deals are a different animal from equity deals. Here, the syndicator is financing the project and earns money from the interest payments made by the developer. In effect, they're acting as the bank to the developer. These interest payments are passed onto you as an investor in the syndicate.

There's a lot to like when it comes to debt crowdfunding. Most regular investors will find this to be a better mode of investment than equity investments. This is because equity investments depend on the sale of the property down the road to generate the bulk of their returns, most of the time.

However, there is no such sale involved when it comes to debt. The developer pays interest to the syndicate and the loan has a fixed term. Once the loan is up, you'll receive your principal back and would have earned interest payments in the interim. Usually, interest is paid on a monthly, quarterly or yearly basis.

Given that these are commercial loans, you'll be receiving interest that is quite high. Usually, the return rates on these investments range from five to 10%. The exact rate of return depends on the interest rate that is provided to the developer. This in turn depends on their credit worthiness.

The less creditworthy the developer is, the higher the interest rate will be. Most platforms have their own credit rating system that runs from A to D, with A being the highest. Some platforms might split these into A1, A2 etc., while some might stick to the full lettering.

As long as you understand what the letters signify, you'll be just fine. These investment opportunities will be across residential and commercial opportunities.

Commercial real estate is riskier than residential real estate as I mentioned earlier, and you'll find that the average rates of return are higher as a result.

Advantages of Crowdfunded Real Estate

There are many advantages that crowdfunded real estate has when compared to REIT investing, and even when compared to physical real estate. Let's look at some of these in detail.

Variety

Crowdfunded projects provide a wide array of investment opportunities. Best of all, you can access these without the need to hire mortgage brokers or contractors. The average investor thinks of rehabbing properties when they look at real estate investment. However, this is a full-time job and the attractive rates of return require you to invest time in generating them.

There are also many things that can go wrong with the project. Crowdfunded real estate brings you the same deals without any of the risks. All you have to do is place your money in them and you're good to go.

Of course, there are risks involved with every deal. Some deals will be duds and will not compensate you adequately for the amount of risk you've run. Other deals might look bad on paper but might work out superbly. At the end of the day, you need to evaluate each on every deal on its merit

However, once you do find a good deal to invest in, you simply sit back and let the syndicator do the work.

Affordability

Much like with REIT investing, crowdfunded real estate gives you access to properties that you might not have access to in real life, thanks to their prohibitive cost. After all, investing in a commercial project's development is expensive. You would stand close to no chance of qualifying for financing for such a project.

Most people struggle to come up with the down payment and closing costs needed to buy a residential project as well since this often runs into low five figures. Crowdfunded real estate removes that barrier. You can invest as little as $100 and buy a unit of these electronic REITs or eREITs.

Flexibility

Crowdfunded real estate has a huge advantage over regular REITs in that you can choose to invest in either a single project or in a portfolio of them. With regular REITs you might love a few projects but be skeptical about a few others. With crowdfunded real estate, this isn't the case.

If you love just one project in the syndicator's portfolio, you can choose to invest in just that project. If you don't wish to invest in equity deals, you can choose to place your money solely in debt deals and so on. You can also narrow your portfolio's focus to the areas you're familiar with.

For example, if you're familiar with the real estate market in Los Angeles, CA, then you can choose to invest your money in properties that are located there. There is no limit to how you can slice and dice your investment strategy.

If all of this is too much of a headache for you then you can simply choose properties from a pre-designed portfolio and invest according to certain objectives. Most online platforms provide investors with portfolios that are geared towards earning income or growth or any other objective.

This sort of flexibility isn't present in REIT investing, and certainly isn't present in physical real estate investing.

Profit Potential

Given that these are private deals, the premium you pay to access them is a lot less. Private markets happen to be more opaque, but the way deals are priced tend to be a lot fairer. Public markets tend to over hype the value of assets in them due to many people speculating in them.

This inflates the price you pay. For example, consider that a company such as Tesla, that has just one quarter of profits, sells at a price that is 209 times its earnings. This is solely because of the hype that its CEO creates on social media and is backed by nothing else. While the company might be successful in the future, does this justify a 209x multiple? Especially when Ford is selling at 27x?

Similarly, public REITs tend to sell at earnings multiples that might be out-of-line with the earnings they're producing. This isn't the case with private REITs since the number of people operating in them are a lot less. This means you're going to receive better prices.

Better prices equal higher potential profits. This is why the average yield of a crowdfunded REIT is higher than the yield on a publicly traded REIT (Bryant, 2020). It isn't that the private REIT pays more money. It's just that, by paying a lower price, the investor receives a higher yield on their investment thanks to fairer pricing.

Risk

Crowdfunded REITs are not traded in the stock market, and as a result, they're not subject to the usual stock market risks. Often REIT prices tend to get depressed when the stock market falls since investors wrongly assume that the entire market is going to tank, when just a portion of it is affected.

For example, if a bank goes under, certain mREITs will also fall in value since both types of companies are a part of the financial sector. This kind of brainless behavior is quite common in the stock market.

By being separate from them, crowdfunded REIT prices don't fluctuate as much and tend to reflect the correct price of the underlying deal. As a result, you as the investor receive fairer prices, as explained previously.

Control and Choice

I touched upon this briefly when highlighting how flexible these investments can be. By providing you with a larger range of investment opportunities, crowdfunded REITs give you immense amounts of choice and control in your investment portfolio. It is something that many real estate investors make use of.

In contrast, REIT investment doesn't give you the same amount of control. Physical real estate does give you control, but it requires a lot of work. Crowdfunded real estate gives you the best of both worlds.

Disadvantages

There are some disadvantages to crowdfunded real estate as well, that you should make a note of. Some of these might result in you staying away from this asset class altogether.

Illiquid

This is the biggest disadvantage of eREITs. They're highly illiquid. While trading on a private market means that your entry price is fair, the same cannot be said for your exit price. Due to the lesser number of people involved in the deal, you'll find a lesser number of people willing to enter at a fair price.

There's another barrier to exiting your investment as well, and this is placed by the syndicator. Often eREITs have redemption schedules and the investor will face lockup periods. In case of extreme market volatility, the syndicator is legally able to freeze redemptions.

For example, the popular crowdfunding platform, Fundrise, recently froze all redemptions thanks to the Covid-19 pandemic. Their fear was that tumbling markets might result in investors redeeming all their shares and as a result, they simply stopped allowing it.

This was painted as the company creating a 'fortress balance sheet,' but one fails to see how they can make such claims by simply not allowing people to access their own money. This was an unpopular move, even if it was the right one from a long-term perspective.

Therefore, a lot of your investment's success depends on the pedigree of the syndicator. You are subject to their whims and fancies. Get stuck with a bad syndicator and you're going to find that exiting your investment will be a headache. This makes choosing the right deal to invest in all the more important.

Return Realization

I mentioned previously how certain deals are marketed to investors as providing a high level of returns. This is often the case in equity deals that involve development of a property. It takes time to build property in the United States, and as a result, you're going to have to wait to see any real returns.

You can choose to stay away from such deals by investing in debt deals. If you choose blended portfolios that conform to a predefined strategy, you will find that it might take a while before you start receiving real cash distributions.

This, coupled with the fact that you can't redeem whenever you choose, makes a lot of investors wary of investing in this asset class. This risk can be mitigated by investing only the money that you can fully afford to lose. This way, you won't be too worried if your investment doesn't pan out the way you expect it to. Most importantly, you'll have the patience to keep holding on to it, even when times get rough.

Due Diligence

These are private companies and the deals aren't offered in the public markets. As a result, your due diligence abilities are limited. As I mentioned earlier, private markets are opaque. While this has a positive effect on how fair prices are, it increases the odds of companies simply making up prices and facts.

I don't mean to say that all deals in private markets are fraudulent. However, the risks are a lot higher. Conducting proper due diligence is a prerequisite for successful investment, and due to the private nature of these markets, you won't be able to do this. The deals you'll have access to will be severely focused on local real estate dynamics.

As a result, you'll need to conduct due diligence into the local real estate market as well. All of this increases the risk of something going wrong, and you'll have to rely on the syndicator completely.

Unsecured

Your investments in crowdfunded real estate is not secure, and you are subject to platform risk. Platform risk refers to how the overall platform is doing. You might have invested in a particular deal, but you're still exposed to the overall platform and the success of all of its other deals.

For example, the platform/syndicator you choose might have invested in 10 deals and you've chosen two successful ones to invest in. If the other eight go bad, your money is going at risk as well since the syndicator's money is tied up in all of these deals. If the other deals exhaust their capital, there's nothing left to pay you.

High LTVs

LTV stands for loan to value, and it's a measure of leverage inherent in a deal. Crowdfunded debt deals usually have LTVs of as much as 95%. In other words, the crowdfunding platform finances 95% of the deal with its own money, with the developer contributing just 5% of the total capital.

This is pretty close to FHA loan LTV ratios, where borrowers pay just three percent down. However, with an FHA loan, the U.S. Government is the one lending the money. They can take a hit or two in terms of defaults. This is not the case with a private lender backing a single property.

Thus, while a debt crowdfunding deal is a better deal for investors, the deal itself tends to be risky because of the high LTV present within it. A high LTV isn't a red flag by any means. It's just that your risk is higher with these deals than with others. A downturn in the market might result in the entire deal crashing down, thanks to having no equity present within it.

The presence of equity, in the form of developer ownership, means that they can still make payments or raise funds through other sources. In high LTV situations, they don't have any money of their own and this puts the entire project on precarious footing. Many deals still go through successfully, but you'll be exposing yourself to economic fluctuations a lot more.

Capital Calls

A lot of these real estate crowdfunding platforms are relatively new and don't have battle-tested managers as yet. As a result, they haven't witnessed too many harsh times. Despite this, a large number of them have called for additional investments from their investors, due to capital shortfalls.

This usually occurs if the syndicator doesn't appraise the property correctly, along with development costs. In the case of equity deals, the repairs needed might be more significant than previously estimated. As a result, more cash is needed to prop the deal up.

Doing this has two possible outcomes for the investor. Either they sink more money into this fund or risk having their existing holdings diluted. After all, the capital base will grow, and if their shareholding remains the same, dilution is the result. Such situations can occur, no matter how strong the capital base of the platform is.

Access

While crowdfunded real estate is largely accessible to all investors, certain deals might be available only to accredited investors. As explained previously, these are individuals or entities who are with more than one million USD when the value of their primary residence is taken out of the equation.

The deals available to regular investors are profitable, but there's no denying that certain lucrative projects tend to be offered to accredited investors because the platform can raise money a lot quicker and in more substantial amounts. Furthermore, the disclosures required when raising money from accredited investors is a lot less.

This makes such offerings a better choice for many platforms. As a result, the ordinary investor misses out.

Choosing Properties

When it comes to choosing the right kinds of properties, pay attention to the level of disclosure the platform provides. A good platform will give you all the information you need to invest successfully. Some of the specific items to look for are:

1. Local market analysis
2. Property investment thesis
3. Cash and return projection
4. LTV disclosures
5. Interest projections
6. Risk disclosures
7. Fees

That last item is something that most investors ignore. Investing in these platforms isn't free. You're going to have to pay fees to access these opportunities. The fee structure varies, depending on the platform and on the type of deals offered. Make sure you study these carefully to understand all the terms involved.

Chapter 6:

Online Investing Platforms

There are two types of platforms you can use to invest in real estate online. If you choose to go down the route of publicly traded REITs, then you'll need to sign up with a stockbroker. This is relatively simple, but you need to be aware of a few legalities. In the case of crowdfunded real estate you'll have to choose an appropriate platform.

Before we dive into those, I'd like to point out that you can invest in physical real estate online as well. Turnkey rental investing has been massively simplified, thanks to companies such as Roofstock. This company provides all relevant data online. Most importantly, it helps you passively invest in opportunities by connecting you to property management companies.

Property management companies take care of your investment and assume all tasks that are related to its smooth functioning. They typically charge between eight to 10% of monthly rent. The 50% rule I highlighted earlier takes property management fees into account.

Visiting the property physically every once in a while is still recommended, of course. However, this is a small-time commitment when you consider that you can invest in a property without leaving the comfort of your home. Roofstock gives you detailed analysis of the neighborhood and of historical property rates.

You can even project your returns and cash flow by using the calculators they have on the website. The platform charges a fee for providing this service, but in this case, it is well worth it. Hiring a good management company is essential when it comes to making your investment in physical real estate passive.

It's a good idea to interview them beforehand, and also ask for references. Don't go for the largest management company by default. They might have a large number of properties, and as a result, yours might be ignored. Keep in mind that you'll have tenants occupying your property, so maintaining it is of paramount importance.

Check the fees associated with management and repairs. Some companies charge you the repairs in full plus labor costs, while others charge a percentage of them. It varies from one company to the next. As a rule of thumb, it's best to hire a company that is local to the area and has experience managing properties there.

This way you can rest assured that an experienced company is taking care of your investment. Once you begin to earn cash from your investment, make sure to accumulate at least six months' worth of rental income in the bank for emergencies. This will help pay for any unforeseen expenses down the road.

REIT and Crowdfunding Platforms

When it comes to finding brokers to invest in REITs, you're spoiled for choice. Here are the things to keep in mind.

Stock Brokers

These days pretty much every broker offers zero-commission trades. Some brokers place minimum balance requirements on their accounts. The likes of Charles Schwab require $25,000, while online brokers such as TD Ameritrade or Firstrade, can be operated with less than $1,000.

There are also apps such as M1 Finance that allow you to invest automatically through preselected portfolio strategies. It's best to stick to tried and tested options instead of any Silicon Valley disruptions. Choose a broker from one of the following:

- TD Ameritrade - Best for beginner investors. Quotes are real time and you can connect your bank accounts directly for funding purposes

- E-Trade - Similar to the above. This company has been around for long and was one of the first brokers to move operations online
- Ally Invest - A great option if you're looking to expand beyond just REITs and into more exotic instruments such as derivatives. Ally Invest makes it easy to invest in options
- Merrill Edge - This is all that remains of the once famous investment bank. It's a bit of a step down from facilitating investment banking deals to facilitating retail stock market trades, but the service is excellent. Some types of accounts might require a minimum investment.

When evaluating such brokers, look for the quality of customer service as well as the presence of zero brokerage fees.

Crowdfunding Platforms

When it comes to evaluating crowdfunding platforms, you need to place a premium on reputation. This is because your money is stuck with them and is illiquid. Here are the best ones to invest with:

- RealtyMogul - The biggest and most popular investment option

- Diversyfund - This is a private REIT and isn't a crowdfunded platform per se. However, it works in the same manner
- Fundrise - One of the current darlings of the space. There is a minimum $500 investment required
- Streitwise - This company offers a few different REITs depending on the kind of exposure you want

Conclusion

Real estate investment is a wonderful way of increasing your net worth, but the minimum investment required can pose a challenge to most investors. In lieu of this, online investment options are a great choice. The best part is that most of these online options don't require high minimum investment amounts.

The most popular investment choice, outside of physical real estate, are REITs. These give you direct exposure to physical property, both in the country as well as internationally. Take the time to analyze and understand how the REIT works before investing money in it.

There are many different kinds of REITs available in the market, and you should take the time to understand what their investment focus is. As you've learned in this book, equity REITs are best suited for the beginner investor, with mREITs posing many risks because of the interest rate volatility.

Crowdfunding is a great way to invest in real estate, but it does have some drawbacks. Chief among them is the fact that your investment is not liquid. You'll be dependent on the platform to redeem your investment, and as a result, you won't have full access to your money whenever you want.

In times of great distress in the economy, redemptions might be frozen to help the fund shore up its assets. Such risks are balanced by the fact that the rewards on offer are generally higher than that of the average publicly traded REIT. Take the time to carefully evaluate the platform you choose to invest in.

While online options exist, sites such as Roofstock enable you to invest in physical real estate remotely. You can make your investment passive by hiring a property management company. While this reduces your overall returns, it does give you the advantages of owning physical property.

Real estate investment is now accessible to investors of all sizes. It doesn't matter how little money you have to invest, you can now partake in the real estate market. This book has given you a number of options, and all that remains for you to do now, is to go ahead and execute your real estate plan.

I wish you the best of luck with all your investment endeavors. Let me know what you think of this book and of everything you've learned in it! Happy investing!

References

Boyte-White, C. (2020, February 18). Our Best Tips for Determining Taxes on Mutual Funds. Investopedia. https://www.investopedia.com/articles/investing/091715/basics-income-tax-mutual-funds.asp

Bryant, S. (2020, January 15). REITs Versus Real Estate Crowdfunding. Investopedia. https://www.investopedia.com/articles/personal-finance/071015/reits-vs-real-estate-crowdfunding-how-they-differ.asp

Case, B. (2017, February 2). Valuing REITs in 2017: Yield Spreads to Treasuries. Nareit. https://www.reit.com/news/blog/market-commentary/valuing-reits-2017-yield-spreads-treasuries#

Chen, J. (2020, September 12). Real Estate Short Sale. Investopedia. https://www.investopedia.com/terms/r/real-estate-short-sale.asp

Frankel, M. (2019, August 6). Real Estate vs. Stocks: Which Has Better Historical Returns?

Millionacres.
https://www.fool.com/millionacres/real-estate-investing/articles/real-estate-vs-stocks-which-has-better-historical-returns/

Historical REIT Spreads: Dividend Yields vs. U.S. Treasuries. (2019, August 22). Millionacres. https://www.fool.com/millionacres/real-estate-investing/reits/reit-investing-101/historical-reit-spreads-dividend-yields-vs-us-treasuries/

Kenton, W. (2019, March 2). Adjusted Funds From Operations (AFFO). Investopedia. https://www.investopedia.com/terms/a/affo.asp

Salzberg, S. (2014, September 1). Do High Voltage Power Lines Cause Cancer? Forbes. https://www.forbes.com/sites/stevensalzberg/2014/09/01/do-high-voltage-power-lines-cause-cancer/#1115947b6497

Stirling, S. (2018, July 15). The 10 N.J. towns faring the worst since the housing crash. NJ. https://www.nj.com/data/2018/07/the_10_nj_towns_faring_the_worst_since_the_housing_crash.html

The Fertility of North American Soils. (2020, June 9). www.ipni.net. http://www.ipni.net/article/IPNI-3030